OFFICIAL

GUIDE TO THE

SMITHSONIAN

Smithsonian Institution Press
Washington, D.C.

Library of Congress Cataloging-in Publication Data
Smithsonian Institution.
Official guide to the Smithsonian.
   p.   cm.
1. Smithsonian Institution–Handbooks, manuals, etc.
I. Title
Q11.S664   1995   069'.09753--dc20   95-24972
ISBN 1-56098-667-0 (alk. paper)

Printed in the United States of America
10 9 8 7 6 5 4 3 2
05 04 03 02 01 00 99

The paper used in this publication meets the minimum
requirements of the American National Standard for
Permanence of Paper for Printed Library Materials
Z39.48-1984.

GUIDEBOOK STAFF
EDITOR: Ellen Cochran Hirzy
PICTURE EDITOR: Anne K. DuVivier
PRODUCTION EDITOR: Heidi M. Lumberg
EXECUTIVE EDITOR: Caroline Newman
PRODUCTION MANAGER: Ken Sabol
DESIGNER: Janice Wheeler

The following are among the many individuals who pro-
vided invaluable assistance in the preparation of this edi-
tion: Susan Biggs, Shireen Dodson, Dru Dowdy, Jane
Gardner, Trish Graboske, Bob Hoage, Janice Kaplan,
Laura Kennedy, Kathy Lindeman, Barbara Livenstein,
Joan Mentzer, Jane McAllister, Mary Patton, Sharon
Reinckens, Daisy Ridgway, Frances Stevenson, Holly
Stewart, Katie Ziglar

Map of the National Mall and building illustrations by
Jamshid Kooros

PHOTO CREDITS:
Mark Avino, Chip Clark, Jessie Cohen, Harold Dorwin,
Bruce Fleischer, Carl Hansen, Alfred Harrell, David
Heald, Franko Khoury, Beth Laakso, Eric Long, Laurie
Minor-Penland, Kim Nielsen, Nicholas J. Parrella, Dane
A. Penland, Charles H. Phillips, Jeffrey Ploskonka,
Carolyn Russo, Lee Stalsworth, Richard Strauss, Jeff
Tinsley, John Tsantes, Rick Vargas, Mark Segal/Folio, Inc.

COVER: The heraldic lion of the Smithsonian Mace, a
symbol of the Smithsonian Institution, holds a sunburst
signifying the power of knowledge. Cover photograph ©
Charles H. Phillips

CONTENTS

WELCOME TO THE SMITHSONIAN

W elcome to the Smithsonian Institution. The year 1996 marks
our sesquicentennial, the Smithsonian's 150th anniversary celebration.
James Smithson's legacy to the United
States, an institution devoted to "the increase and diffusion of knowledge," has
been fulfilled in ways he could not have
imagined.

When you visit the Smithsonian, you
will discover an institution that is unique
in all the world. It is not, as many visitors
expect, simply a museum, or even a clus-
ter of museums. Instead, it is a vast national research and educational center that
encompasses—in addition to its exhibition halls and art galleries—laboratories,
observatories, field stations, scientific expeditions, classrooms, performing arts
events, publications, and more. And it be-
longs, in all its glorious diversity, to the
people of the United States.

The last century and a half have brought
enormous growth to the Institution and a
distinctive character to its mission, as the
Smithsonian has expanded from a lone Castle building where bison roamed an outside pen to an extensive museum and research complex that today includes 16 museums, the National Zoological Park,
and research centers in eight states and the Republic
of Panama. The Institution is the steward for some
140 million objects, which form the basis of research, exhibitions, and public programs in the arts,
history, and the sciences. The scope of the Smithsonian reminds me of the breadth and depth of a
great university.

For 15 decades, the Institution has stayed true to
its mission. In doing so, however, it continually
strives to adapt to the changing social and physical

environment, to the fast-paced growth of technology, and to the shifting interests and concerns of the American people. Witness some of our achievements: the annual Festival of American Folklife, which explores living national and international cultures; the innovative Amazonia rainforest exhibit at the National Zoo; the presentation of the nation's accomplishments in science and technology; the systematic collection and examination of the world's biological specimens; and the restoration and preservation of national treasures such as the Star-Spangled Banner and other irreplaceable works of American art and culture.

Our 150th anniversary represents a chance not only to celebrate our past achievements, but to look to the future as we forge exciting new directions. The Smithsonian will continue to sustain its vibrant program of exhibitions and educational activities on the National Mall. The newest addition to the Smithsonian family, the National Museum of the American Indian, is scheduled to open in Washington early in the 21st century.

At the same time, we are increasingly committed to harnessing advanced information technologies to take the Smithsonian into American homes and schools through diverse media such as the Internet and CD-ROM. I am particularly excited by what this technology can mean to us in extending the reach of our historic mission—the increase and diffusion of knowledge. At the heart of the information revolution is something more than advanced technology. It is the fulfillment of one central promise of democracy: to make knowledge available to as many citizens as possible and to allow their needs to shape that access. I see it as James Smithson's mandate reborn for a new century and a new generation.

In this guide you will find descriptions of the various objects and exhibitions throughout our museums. Historical treasures, significant scientific specimens, magnificent works of art—all are at the Smithsonian for you to learn from and enjoy. Not to be overlooked are the animals, including rare and endangered species, at the National Zoo. We hope this guide enhances your visit, whether you are discovering the Smithsonian for the first time—or the 150th!

I. Michael Heyman
Secretary
Smithsonian Institution

THE SMITHSONIAN AT A GLANCE

The Smithsonian Institution is a complex of 16 museums, the National Zoological Park, and numerous research facilities. Fourteen museums and the Zoo are located in Washington, D.C. Cooper-Hewitt National Design Museum and the George Gustav Heye Center of the National Museum of the American Indian are in New York City.

Here is some basic information to help you plan your Smithsonian visit.

ADMISSION

Admission is free to all Washington Smithsonian museums, the National Zoo, and the George Gustav Heye Center of the National Museum of the American Indian in New York.

HOURS

Most Smithsonian museums are open daily except December 25 from 10 a.m. to 5:30 p.m. (Check museum listings in this guide.) Extended spring and summer hours are determined each year. At the Zoo, buildings are open year-round from 9 a.m. to 4:30 p.m. (unless otherwise posted); the grounds are open from 8 a.m. to 8 p.m. (April 15–October 15) and 8 a.m. to 6 p.m. (October 16–April 14).

HOW TO GET THERE

We recommend using public transportation, including taxis, when visiting Washington's attractions. The Metrorail subway system and Metrobus link the downtown area with nearby communities in Maryland and Virginia. To locate the Metrorail station nearest the museum you want to visit, see the museum listings in this guide. For more information, call Metro at (202) 637-7000 (voice); (202) 638-3780 (TTY for callers with communication impairments).

Because the Smithsonian is a growing, changing institution, the exhibitions described in this guide are subject to change. Special temporary exhibitions also come and go from the museums. Please inquire about current exhibitions and programs at the Smithsonian Information Center in the Castle or at museum information desks, or call (202) 357-2700; TTY: (202) 357-1729 (for callers with communication impairments).

• The Smithsonian Institution Building—the colorful red sandstone Castle on the Mall—symbolizes the Smithsonian to many visitors. The building's Great Hall houses the Smithsonian Information Center.

• BELOW: Visitors entering the Castle on the south side, from Independence Avenue, can first stroll through the Enid A. Haupt Garden.

• OPPOSITE TOP: A visitor uses one of the interactive touch screens in the Smithsonian Information Center.

• OPPOSITE BOTTOM: The Smithsonian's Festival of American Folklife celebrates America's splendidly diverse cultural heritage. Traditional music and craftspeople from all over the nation and abroad attract visitors by the thousands to the Mall each year.

The Smithsonian does not operate public parking facilities. Limited restricted street parking is available on and around the National Mall; posted times are enforced. Some commercial parking can be found in the area.

SMITHSONIAN INFORMATION CENTER

Open daily at 9 a.m. in the Castle, the Smithsonian's first building, the center has a multifaceted information and orientation program. Volunteer information specialists can answer questions and give directions until 4 p.m. Information is provided in Arabic, Chinese, English, French, German, Japanese, and Spanish. *Smithsonian Access*, a free guide for visitors with disabilities, is available on request. Visit, write, or call: Smithsonian Information Center, Smithsonian Institution, SI Building, Room 153, MRC 010, Washington, D.C. 20560; (202) 357-2700 (voice); (202) 357-1729 (TTY for callers with communication impairments). For daily 24-hour recorded activity information, call Dial-a-Museum: (202) 357-2020 (English); (202) 633-9126 (Spanish).

ONLINE INFORMATION

A wealth of information about the Smithsonian and its resources is available through the Smithsonian Home Page on the World Wide Web at *http://www.si.edu*. Commercial online services also offer Smithsonian information. See page 192 for more information about Smithsonian electronic resources.

PHOTOGRAPHY

Hand-held and video cameras are permitted for personal use in all museums. Photography is prohib-

ited, as posted, in some exhibitions. At the Renwick Gallery and the National Museum of American Art, you may photograph only the permanent collections. You may not use flash attachments in the Hirshhorn Museum and the National Museum of African Art. The use of tripods is prohibited in all buildings. Exceptions to these rules may occur in any exhibition or building.

PETS

With the exception of certified-assistance animals, pets are not permitted in any of the museums or at the Zoo.

WHERE TO EAT

Food service is available in the National Air and Space Museum, the National Museum of American History, and the National Museum of Natural History. (Food service facilities at the National Museum of Natural History will close for renovation from April 1996 through July 1998.) An outdoor café is open during warm-weather months at the Hirshhorn Museum. The National Museum of American Art/National Portrait Gallery building has a small café. The Zoo has a variety of fast-food services.

MUSEUM SHOPS

Located in most Smithsonian museums, the shops carry books, crafts, graphics, jewelry, reproductions, toys, and gifts that relate to the museums' collections. The Arts and Industries Building shop features Smithsonian mail-order catalogue items.

SIGHTSEEING TOURS

Tourmobile, the only commercial sightseeing service federally authorized to operate on the National Mall, offers narrated tours with stops at Smithsonian museums, major memorials and monuments, government and historic buildings, and Arlington National Cemetery. Fees include reboarding options. For recorded information, call (202) 554-5100. Information subject to change. Verify by calling Smithsonian Information.

THE
NATIONAL
MALL

Along, open, grassy stretch from the Capitol to the Washington Monument, the original Mall was an important feature of Pierre L'Enfant's 1791 plan for the city of Washington. He envisioned it as a "vast esplanade" lined with grand residences. Before the Smithsonian Institution Building (the Castle) was built in the mid-19th century, however, the Mall was used mainly for grazing and gardens. To the west, beyond the spot where the Washington Monument now stands, were tidal flats and marshes. After these areas were gradually filled, the Mall was officially extended in the 20th century to the Lincoln Memorial.

In 1850 New York horticulturist Andrew Jackson Downing was commissioned to landscape the Mall. But his design, which called for curving carriage drives amid a grove of American evergreens, was only partly realized. By 1900 the Mall had deteriorated. Its eyesores included a railroad station with sheds, tracks, and coal piles. Two years later, work was begun to implement L'Enfant's early concept. Over the years much of his vision has become reality on a National Mall distinguished by rows of great museum buildings.

On the Mall today, people jog, fly kites, toss frisbees, or just stroll. Near the Castle, children ride on an old-fashioned carousel. For a time each summer, the colorful Festival of American Folklife fills the Mall with traditional music and crafts. On the benches alongside the walkways, visitors rest while deciding which Smithsonian museum to explore next.

•OVERLEAF: Artist Jamshid Kooros captures the historic core of the Smithsonian museum complex in this delightful rendering of the National Mall.

ABOUT THE
SMITHSONIAN

Metro station: Smithsonian

For information about the Smithsonian,

call (202) 357-2700, or TTY (202) 357-1729.

For daily 24-hour recorded information, call Dial-a-Museum,

(202) 357-2020 (English); (202) 633-9126 (Spanish).

For many people, the red sandstone building that resembles a castle symbolizes the Smithsonian Institution. But the Smithsonian is much more. It encompasses 16 museums, the National Zoological Park, and numerous research facilities. Centered on the National Mall in Washington, D.C., the Smithsonian's presence extends to other parts of the Nation's Capital and to eight states and the Republic of Panama.

First of all, the Smithsonian Institution is the world's largest museum complex, with collections in every area of human interest numbering more than 140 million items. The objects in Smithsonian museums range from a magnificent collection of ancient Chinese bronzes to Judy Garland's ruby slippers from *The Wizard of Oz*, from memorabilia of the U.S. presidency to the Apollo lunar landing module to a 3.5-billion-year-old fossil. The scope is staggering. All of these objects help us understand the past, consider the present, and preserve history for future generations.

Only a small part of the Smithsonian's collections are on display in the museums at any one time. Scholars and scientists use the rest behind the scenes as they work to increase our knowledge of science, art, and history. The Smithsonian is also one of the world's leading research centers. On expeditions to all parts of the world, Smithsonian scientists gather new facts and specimens. Smithsonian publications

Begin your Smithsonian visit at the Smithsonian Information Center in the Smithsonian Institution Building (the Castle) on the Mall, open daily except December 25 from 9 a.m. to 5:30 p.m.

make available the information that these experts assemble.

A CENTER FOR LEARNING

The Smithsonian is deeply involved in public education for people of all ages. Visiting groups of schoolchildren are a common sight in the museums, and families come together on weekend outings and summer vacations. Educators from the elementary school through the university level use the Smithsonian's resources, as do scholars pursuing advanced research. Through The Smithsonian Associates, adults and children enjoy classes, lectures, studio arts courses, and a variety of other educational activities.

The Smithsonian also offers an exciting schedule of "living exhibits." Performing arts activities include music, theater, dance, film programs, and Discovery Theater performances for young people. The popular Festival of American Folklife, a celebration of the nation's rich cultural heritage, brings musicians and craftspeople to the Mall each summer.

• The skies fill with a rainbow of colors each spring, as flyers from around the world join Smithsonian Associates at the Kite Festival on the Mall.

As a national institution, the Smithsonian takes cultural and educational programs to people across the country. The Smithsonian Institution Traveling Exhibition Service develops and circulates exhibitions to many communities. *Smithsonian* and *Air & Space/Smithsonian* magazines publish lively articles on topics inspired by Smithsonian activities. The Smithsonian Associates sponsor lectures, research expeditions, and other events nationwide. Books and recordings from Smithsonian Institution Press as well as documentaries for cable and public television, videos, radio programs, and educational media bring the Smithsonian into millions of homes. Through the Internet and commercial online services, home and school computer users have instant access to a rich resource with which to plan a visit, find out about programs and exhibitions, and even communicate online with Smithsonian museums.

RESEARCH AT THE SMITHSONIAN

The Smithsonian's research activities are known throughout the world for their benefit to the scholarly community and to the advancement of knowledge. Smithsonian scientists, historians, and art historians explore topics as diverse as global environmental concerns, the nature of the world's changing human and social systems, and the care and preservation of museum objects.

ARCHIVES OF AMERICAN ART

The Archives collects and preserves materials documenting the history of the visual arts in the United States. Regional centers are located in New York, Boston, Detroit, Los Angeles, and Washington, D.C. For information, call (202) 357-2781.

CONSERVATION ANALYTICAL LABORATORY

Scientists at this facility, located at the Smithsonian's Museum Support Center in Suitland, Maryland, use the latest technology to carry out research in the technical study, analysis, and conservation of museum objects. Not open to the public.

CONSERVATION AND RESEARCH CENTER, NATIONAL ZOOLOGICAL PARK

This 1,255-hectare (3,100-acre) wooded area in the foothills of the Blue Ridge Mountains in Front Royal, Virginia, is a breeding preserve and study center for the National Zoo's rare and endangered animals. Not open to the public.

MARINE STATION AT LINK PORT

Scientists working at this research center located in Fort Pierce, Florida, study estuarine and marine environments along Florida's east coastline and adjacent ocean shelves, seeking basic information about natural and human causes of stress and environmental change. The station is operated by the National Museum of Natural History. For information, call (407) 465-6630.

SMITHSONIAN ASTROPHYSICAL OBSERVATORY

At this organization, part of the Harvard University–Smithsonian Center for Astrophysics in Cambridge, Massachusetts, scientists study the physical characteristics and evolution of the universe. The largest field facility is the Fred Lawrence Whipple Observatory on Mount Hopkins near Tucson, Arizona. Among the research instruments there is the world's first Multiple Mirror Telescope, developed jointly with the University of Arizona. For information about public programs in Cambridge, call (617) 495-7461; at the Whipple Observatory, call (602) 670-5707.

SMITHSONIAN ENVIRONMENTAL RESEARCH CENTER

Staff and visiting researchers at this center near the Chesapeake Bay study land-water relationships and plan public programs to increase awareness of ecological systems and determine how they are affected by human disturbance. For information about public programs, call (301) 261-4190 (from the Washington area) or (410) 798-4424 (from other areas).

SMITHSONIAN TROPICAL RESEARCH INSTITUTE

Scientists from the Smithsonian and all over the world study the evolution and behavior of tropical organisms at various facilities of this institute in the Republic of Panama. For information, call (507) 27-6022.

HISTORY OF THE SMITHSONIAN

The Smithsonian owes its origin to James Smithson, a British scientist who never visited the United States. Smithson named his nephew Henry James Hungerford as the beneficiary in his will. He stipulated that should Hungerford die without heirs (as he did in 1835), the entire Smithson fortune would go to this country. The purpose would be to found "at Washington, under the name of the Smithsonian Institution, an establishment for the increase and diffusion of knowledge."

On July 1, 1836, Congress accepted Smithson's legacy and pledged the faith of the United States to the charitable trust. In 1838, after British courts had approved the bequest, the nation received Smithson's estate—bags of gold sovereigns, then the equivalent of more than half a million dollars, a great fortune in those days. Eight years later, on August 10, 1846, President James K. Polk signed an Act of Congress establishing the Smithsonian Institution in its present form and providing for the administration of the Smithson trust, independent of the government, by a board of regents and secretary of the Smithsonian. With the formal creation of the Smithsonian came a commitment to the work that continues today in research, museum and library operation, and the dissemination of information in science, art, and history.

Today, the Smithsonian is a national institution that receives a substantial appropriation from the federal government. Essential funding also comes from private sources, including the Smithson trust, other endowments, individuals, foundations, corporations, and revenues raised from such activities as membership programs, a mail-order catalogue, museum shops, food services, and the Smithsonian Institution Press.

The chief executive officer of the Smithsonian is

• TOP: Technicians, using research chambers on a tidal marsh near the Chesapeake Bay, monitor plants exposed to increased levels of carbon dioxide, a greenhouse gas that contributes to global warming.

• BOTTOM: A 100-foot-high crane looming above the rainforest in Panama's Parque Metropolitano lowers Tropical Research Institute scientists to different levels of the canopy for measuring temperature and humidity.

SMITHSONIAN SECRETARIES: 1846 TO TODAY

JOSEPH HENRY, a famous physical scientist and a pioneer and inventor in electricity, was founding secretary from 1846 until his death in 1878. Henry set the Smithsonian's course with an emphasis on science.

SPENCER FULLERTON BAIRD, a naturalist, served from 1878 until his death in 1887. Baird developed the early Smithsonian museums and promoted the accumulation of natural history specimens and collections of all kinds.

SAMUEL PIERPONT LANGLEY, whose particular interests were aeronautics, astrophysics, and astronomy, launched the Smithsonian in those directions during his years in office, from 1887 to 1906.

CHARLES DOOLITTLE WALCOTT, a geologist and paleontologist, was secretary from 1907 to 1927. During his administration, the National Museum of Natural History opened to the public, and the National Collection of Fine Arts (now the National Museum of American Art) and the Freer Gallery of Art joined the Smithsonian.

CHARLES GREELEY ABBOT, secretary from 1928 to 1944, was a specialist in solar radiation and solar power. He established a bureau to study the effect of light on plant and animal life, the precursor to the Smithsonian Environmental Research Center.

ALEXANDER WETMORE, an ornithologist, succeeded Abbot in 1945. During his tenure, the National Air Museum and the Canal Biological Area (now the Smithsonian Tropical Research Institute) became part of the Institution.

LEONARD CARMICHAEL, a physiological psychologist and former Tufts University president, held office between 1953 and 1964. During those years, the National Museum of History and Technology (now the National Museum of American History) opened.

S. DILLON RIPLEY, biologist, ecologist, and authority on birds of the Far East, served from 1964 to 1984. Under his leadership the Smithsonian expanded, adding the Hirshhorn Museum and Sculpture Garden, the National Museum of African Art, the Renwick Gallery, and Cooper-Hewitt National Design Museum. The National Air and Space Museum moved to its present building, and construction began on the underground complex for the National Museum of African Art and the Arthur M. Sackler Gallery. Ripley also encouraged innovative ways of serving a wider public.

ROBERT McC. ADAMS, an anthropologist, archaeologist, and university administrator, served from 1984 to 1994. During his time as secretary, the Smithsonian placed new emphasis on broader involvement of diverse cultural communities and focused on enhancing research support and education outreach. The National Museum of the American Indian was established as part of the Smithsonian during Adams's administration.

I. MICHAEL HEYMAN, the current secretary, is a law professor and former chancellor of the University of California at Berkeley. During his tenure at Berkeley, he strengthened the university's biosciences departments and successfully promoted ethnic diversification of the undergraduate student body while maintaining high academic standards. His distinguished teaching career includes posts at Yale and Stanford universities. Most recently, Heyman was counselor to the secretary of the interior and deputy assistant secretary for policy.

the secretary. The institution is governed by a board of regents, which by law is composed of the vice president of the United States, the chief justice of the United States, three members of the Senate, three members of the House of Representatives, and

nine private citizens. The chief justice has traditionally served as chancellor of the Smithsonian.

Each museum has its own director and staff. The central administration of the Smithsonian is headquartered in the Castle building.

THE CASTLE

The red sandstone Smithsonian Institution Building, popularly known as the Castle, symbolizes the entire institution to many visitors. It was designed in Norman style (a 12th-century combination of late Romanesque and early Gothic motifs) by James Renwick Jr., architect of Grace Church and St. Patrick's Cathedral in New York and the Renwick Gallery of the National Museum of American Art in Washington.

A disastrous fire in 1865—just 10 years after the Castle was completed—caused extensive damage and the loss of valuable objects. Restoration of the building took two years. In the 1880s much of the Castle was remodeled and enlarged. In recent years

many of its rooms have been restored and furnished with Victorian period furniture.

The Castle originally housed the entire Smithsonian, including a science museum, lecture hall, art gallery, research laboratories, administrative offices, and living quarters for the secretary and his family. Today, administrative offices and the Smithsonian Information Center are located there. The Information Center opens daily (except December 25) at 9 a.m.

ENID A. HAUPT GARDEN AND S. DILLON RIPLEY CENTER

Behind the Castle is a magnificent parklike garden named for its donor, philanthropist Enid Annenberg Haupt. Changing with the seasons, it features exquisite trees, plants, and flowers. In the center is a large 19th-century parterre. Throughout the garden are pieces of Victorian garden furniture, some from the early days of the Castle and the Arts and Industries Building.

Beneath the Haupt Garden is a three-level underground museum, research, and education complex that contains the Arthur M. Sackler Gallery, the National Museum of African Art, and the S. Dillon Ripley Center. The museums are accessible through above-ground entrance pavilions. Through a bronze-domed kiosk, visitors enter the Ripley Center, named for the Smithsonian's eighth secretary. It houses the International Gallery with its changing exhibitions; workshops and classrooms for public programs; and a lecture hall. The Smithsonian Associates and the Smithsonian Institution Traveling Exhibition Service have their offices in the Ripley Center.

• ABOVE: **Willard Scott hosts young visitors on NBC's *Today Show* during the Smithsonian's annual Kite Festival on the Mall.**

• OPPOSITE TOP AND BOTTOM: **Young visitors examine some of the Discovery Room's many touchable specimens at the National Museum of Natural History.**

NATIONAL AIR AND SPACE MUSEUM

The National Air and Space Museum offers a range of programs for families, children, and school groups. Tours, lectures, workshops, films, and performances are scheduled throughout the year. Call the Tour and Reservation Office, (202) 357-1504, or ask at the Information Desk for an advance schedule and the posted events for the day. Children especially enjoy the spectacular films on flight and the environment shown on the five-story-high screen in the Langley Theater. The Albert Einstein Planetarium features lectures on the night sky and multimedia programs on astronomy and space. Both have admission fees.

NATIONAL MUSEUM OF NATURAL HISTORY

After you marvel at the dinosaurs, the gems and minerals, and the exhibit on giant squids, you can enjoy a variety of participatory activities. In the O. Orkin Insect Zoo, you can crawl through a model of a termite mound, look into a real beehive, or hold some of the insects in the zoo. Popular tarantula feedings take place three times a day. The Discovery Room (first floor) is a family-oriented education center where visitors can touch, feel, smell, and taste objects from the world of nature. For hours and other information, see the museum listing in this guide. Note: In 1998, this facility will move to a 4,000-square-foot area on the top level of the new Discovery Center.

NATIONAL MUSEUM OF AMERICAN HISTORY

In the Hands On Science Center ("Science in American Life" exhibition, first floor), you can experience the fun and excitement of experimental science. Activities for visitors ages five and older include testing for food additives and finding out the ultraviolet rating for your sunglasses.

In the Information Interactive Gallery ("Information Age" exhibition, first floor) try interactive demonstrations and activities, such as having your fingerprints taken and enciphering your name with the German ENIGMA encoder.

Touch, examine, and use objects similar to those elsewhere in the museum when you visit the Hands On History Room (near the Star-Spangled Banner, second floor). Visitors ages five and older can try more than 30 activities. Young children especially enjoy unpacking Betsy's Moving Trunk, which lets them learn about life on a Virginia plantation in the 1780s.

During the week after Christmas, the museum stages a Holiday Celebration, with singing, dancing, baking, crafts, and beautifully decorated trees.

FREER GALLERY OF ART AND ARTHUR M. SACKLER GALLERY

Programs for young visitors include ImaginAsia, which uses an adult-child self-guided art tour as inspiration for a project that children may create with help from the education staff. Activity guides for some exhibitions also help family groups enjoy the gallery together.

NATIONAL MUSEUM OF AFRICAN ART

The museum introduces children to traditional African arts and cultures through participatory workshops, storytelling, musical performances, and other activities. Programs for children and families are often offered in conjunction with special exhibitions.

HIRSHHORN MUSEUM AND SCULPTURE GARDEN

Children accompanied by adults can explore the Hirshhorn with the museum's *Family Guide* or join "Young at Art" programs on select Saturday mornings for interactive gallery visits and hands-on workshops. Family film programs are presented at 11 a.m. most Saturdays from October through May. "Currents," an in-depth, daylong seminar for teenagers using art at the Hirshhorn as a basis for broader cultural studies, is presented twice a year. A stroll through the Sculpture Garden is another popular family activity.

NATIONAL PORTRAIT GALLERY

Tours for families with children are offered daily at the National Portrait Gallery. Ask at the Information Desk, where a self-guide is also available. Docent-led tours of the gallery, and other programs designed for school groups of 10 or more students, are outlined in the *School Services Brochure*.

NATIONAL MUSEUM OF AMERICAN ART

Many works in the museum's permanent collection and special exhibitions are especially appealing for children, in-

Smithsonian museums offer an array of special events and programs for children and families throughout the year. For current information, call the museum directly or check at the information desk.

• LEFT: Visitors to the American Indian Museum's Heye Center use interactive technology to learn more about the Native peoples of the Americas.

• BELOW: All eyes are on the stage during a performance in the Discovery Theater, Arts and Industries Building.

cluding the lively folk art selections and paintings and sculpture depicting Native Americans in the first floor galleries. The museum conducts special tours for children by appointment. Family days featuring music, dance, writing, and gallery activities are offered in conjunction with special exhibitions.

NATIONAL POSTAL MUSEUM

This museum is designed for a family audience, with state-of-the-art interactive displays, inviting exhibit design, and activities geared to adults and children. Try some of the 30 audiovisual and interactive areas, the three computer games, and the computer kiosk where you can address, meter, and send personalized postcards.

Participatory displays invite you to travel on the first postal road, open a mailbag, or sort the mail. In the Discovery Center, you can play with Activity Mail Boxes filled with games, puzzles, and hands-on adventures.

ANACOSTIA MUSEUM

Family activities at this museum include music, storytelling, festivals, and events held in conjunction with special exhibitions. At the annual Juneteenth celebration, held to commemorate the emancipation of Texas slaves, families enjoy music, games, demonstrations, and food on the museum grounds.

NATIONAL ZOO

The giant panda, big cats, elephants, great apes, and reptiles are Zoo favorites for children of all ages. To

see Hsing-Hsing, the panda, when he is most active, visit during feeding times at 11 a.m. outdoors (weather permitting) and 3 p.m. indoors. Daily at 11:30 a.m., you can observe elephant health care in the Elephant House or watch a seal and sea lion feeding and training demonstration.

In the Amazonia rainforest exhibit, explore specimens and artifacts in the biologist's field station. The Reptile Discovery Center features hands-on activities and the chance to see endangered Komodo dragons, the world's largest lizards.

ZOOlab and the Bird Resource Center are good places to discover more about the animals by exploring, looking, touching, and reading. ZOOlab in the Education Building and the Bird Resource Center in the Bird House are open Friday through Sunday from 10 a.m. to 1 p.m.

NATIONAL MUSEUM OF THE AMERICAN INDIAN GEORGE GUSTAV HEYE CENTER

Public programs such as Talking Circles and Native American Expressive Culture introduce children to native music, dance, media arts, visual

• Young Smithsonian Associates gather for an afternoon of learning and fun at the Natural History Museum's delightful butterfly garden.

arts, theater, storytelling, and oratory. In the Resource Center, adults and children can learn more about the museum—as well as native life and history—using the latest computer technology.

CAROUSEL ON THE MALL

As a perfect break from museums for adults and children, ride the carousel on the National Mall near the Arts and Industries Building. It operates from 11 a.m. to 5 p.m. on weekdays and from 10 a.m. to 6 p.m. on weekends, weather permitting. There is a small fee.

DISCOVERY THEATER

This popular theater for young audiences presents live performances by storytellers, puppeteers, dancers, actors, and singers. For show times, tickets, and reservations, call (202) 357-1500 (voice and TTY) between 10 a.m. and 4 p.m. weekdays.

THE SMITHSONIAN ASSOCIATES

Imaginative programs inspired by Smithsonian museums are offered all year long for children and families through the Resident Associate program. For information, call (202) 357-3030.

TIPS FOR VISITING THE SMITHSONIAN WITH CHILDREN

1. Plan ahead.
Before your visit, call Smithsonian information at (202) 357-2700 or (202) 357-1729 (TTY), and ask for the "family package." Or drop by the Information Center in the Castle.

2. The Smithsonian adventure
Make your visit to the Smithsonian an adventure for your kids by talking about the things they will see. A bedtime story about dinosaurs or the Wright brothers will build the excitement.

3. Children first
A child's attention span can be very short. One way to keep a youngster interested in museum exhibits and activities is to focus your visit on what the child wants to do.

4. Do you know why. . .?
Another way to keep a child interested is to talk about the exhibits you are visiting. For example, at the National Museum of American Art, you could ask what your youngster thinks about the way children dressed 200 years ago compared to the way we dress today.

5. More than meets the eye
For a change of pace, visit a "discovery" room or a hands-on exhibit area. Ask at any museum information desk about special performances, storytelling sessions, or workshops. Or try one of the many interactive computers, like the ones in the National Museum of American History's "Information Age" and "Science in American Life" exhibitions.

6. Time out!
Take frequent breaks, especially when visiting with preschoolers. The museum shops have a great selection of children's books, especially at the National Museum of American History and the National Museum of Natural History. Stop by one of the museum cafeterias or the Ice Cream Parlor in the American History Museum for a treat. Or enjoy a family picnic outdoors on the National Mall.

NATIONAL
AIR AND SPACE
MUSEUM

Independence Avenue at 6th Street, SW

Mall entrance: Jefferson Drive at 6th Street, SW

Open daily except December 25, 10 a.m. to 5:30 p.m.

(Extended spring and summer hours determined annually)

Metro station: L'Enfant Plaza

Smithsonian information: (202) 357-2700

Information recording in Spanish: (202) 633-9126

TTY: (202) 357-1729 (for callers with communication impairments)

Young or old, flight buff or harried tourist, everyone who has walked through the National Air and Space Museum has shared a distinctive and memorable experience. The museum has a vast assemblage of aircraft, spacecraft, and related artifacts for visitors to see, but the experience involves more than that. There is a sense of history relived, horizons expanded, optimism rekindled, pride reborn, wonder renewed.

NATIONAL AIR AND SPACE MUSEUM

? Information   ¶¶ Food Service

⊞ Stairs/Escalators   🛍 Museum Shop

☒ Elevators   ♿ Wheelchair Entrance

👫 Restrooms

FIRST FLOOR

Mall entrance

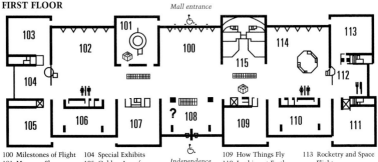

103 | 102 | 101 | 100 | 114 | 113
104 | | | 115 | | 112
105 | 106 | 107 | 108 | 109 | 110 | 111

Independence Avenue entrance

100 Milestones of Flight
101 Museum Shop
102 Air Transportation
103 Dream to Fly: The Black Experience in Aviation (opening 1998–99)
104 Special Exhibits
105 Golden Age of Flight
106 Jet Aviation
107 Early Flight
108 South Lobby
109 How Things Fly
110 Looking at Earth
111 Stars
112 Lunar Exploration Vehicles
113 Rocketry and Space Flight
114 Space Hall
115 Samuel P. Langley Theater

SECOND FLOOR

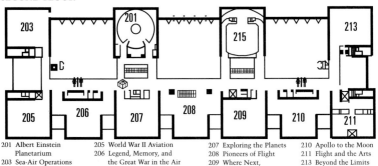

203 | 201 | 215 | 213
205 | 206 | 207 | 208 | 209 | 210 | 211

201 Albert Einstein Planetarium
203 Sea-Air Operations
205 World War II Aviation
206 Legend, Memory, and the Great War in the Air
207 Exploring the Planets
208 Pioneers of Flight
209 Where Next, Columbus?
210 Apollo to the Moon
211 Flight and the Arts
213 Beyond the Limits
215 Theater

NOTE: The Educational Resource Center for teachers is located on the parking level. It can be entered via the escalator in the South Lobby.

•**PRECEDING PAGES: A** view of the Milestones of Flight gallery, displaying aircraft and spacecraft that have made aviation history. The Wright Flyer hangs from the ceiling.

•**RIGHT:** *Delta Solar*, by sculptor Alejandro Otero, was a Bicentennial gift from the Venezuelan government. The large delta-shaped structure is filled with stainless steel rotary sails that turn in the breeze.

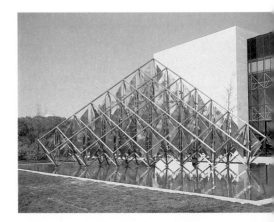

INFORMATION DESK

In the Independence Avenue lobby

TOURS

Public tours are offered daily at 10:15 a.m. and 1 p.m.; no advance reservations are needed. Tours for school groups (25 to 125 people) and other organizations must be scheduled at least three weeks in advance. Call (202) 357-1400; TTY: (202) 357-1505 or 357-1696.

FREE SCIENCE DEMONSTRATIONS

A daily schedule is posted at the Information Desk.

WHERE TO EAT

A full-service restaurant—the Wright Place—and the Flight Line Cafeteria are located on the first floor, east end.

MUSEUM SHOPS

Near the Mall entrance and on the second floor. Books, postcards, slides, posters, models, souvenirs, T-shirts, and first-day stamp covers are for sale.

FILMS AND PLANETARIUM SHOWS

Films on flight and the environment are projected on a huge screen in the Samuel P. Langley Theater, with continuous showings daily. The Albert Einstein Planetarium also has presentations daily. There is a nominal admission fee for films and planetarium shows.

EDUCATIONAL SERVICES

Information on daily events for children and families is available at the Information Desk or by calling (202) 357-1504. The museum offers workshops, orientations, and a resource center to help teachers and professional educators use the museum as a resource. Ask for a program brochure and other information at the Information Desk.

• *Continuum*, a bronze sculpture by Charles O. Perry, stands outside the Independence Avenue entrance

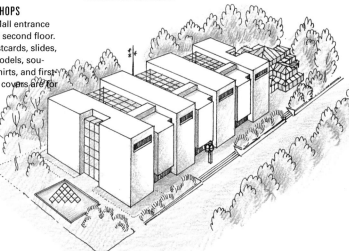

AT A GLANCE

The Wright brothers' **1903 Flyer**, Charles Lindbergh's *Spirit of St. Louis*, John Glenn's *Friendship 7*, the **Apollo 11 command module,** and the walk-through **Skylab orbital workshop**: these are just a few of the attractions in this vast and exciting museum. Not to be missed are special films on flight and the environment, projected on a screen five stories high and seven stories wide, providing a breathtaking cinematic experience.

The museum tells the story of aeronautics and spaceflight in 23 galleries, each devoted to a subject or theme. Visitors are surrounded by visual excitement—theaters, multimedia shows, dioramas, interactive computers, and many innovative exhibits. Overhead and all around are aircraft, rockets, and spacecraft on display.

The museum has more than 360 historic or technologically significant aircraft, about 300 rockets and spacecraft, and hundreds of engines, propellers, scale models, aviation uniforms, space suits, awards, works of art, instruments, flight equipment, and other items. Although much of the collection is on display, many artifacts are stored at the Paul E. Garber Preservation, Restoration, and Storage Facility (see page 48), and a significant number are on loan to other museums.

Nearly all the aircraft and most of the spacecraft in the galleries are genuine. When it is not possible to exhibit a particular spacecraft (since many cannot be recovered once launched), the backup vehicle is shown or a replica is made from authentic flight hardware. Satellites and space probes are flight backup or test vehicles, as similar to the orig-

• ABOVE LEFT: The Apollo lunar module, the backup to the first lunar module flown in orbit and similar to Apollo 11's *Eagle*

• ABOVE RIGHT: This detail from Robert McCall's mural *Space Mural—A Cosmic View*, on view in the lobby, shows an Apollo astronaut standing triumphantly on the Moon's surface holding the American flag.

• OPPOSITE: Apollo 11 command module *Columbia* carried astronauts Neil Armstrong, Buzz Aldrin, and Michael Collins to the Moon and back in July 1969.

inals as possible. Labels specifically note these distinctions.

The logical place to start a tour of the museum is the Milestones of Flight gallery at the Mall entrance.

GALLERY 100—MILESTONES OF FLIGHT

Famous airplanes and spacecraft that are historical milestones are displayed on two visual levels.

HIGHLIGHTS—GROUND LEVEL

Mercury *Friendship* 7—First U.S. manned orbital flight, 1962

Gemini IV—First U.S. space walk, 1965; space suits worn by astronauts Edward H. White and James A. McDivitt

Apollo 11 command module *Columbia*—First lunar landing mission, 1969; astronaut Michael Collins's space suit

Touchable Moon rock—Collected by Apollo 17 astronauts from the lunar surface

Viking Lander—Proof-test vehicle for the first spacecraft to study in detail the surface of another planet (Mars), 1976

Goddard rockets—Full-scale model of the world's first liquid propellant rocket (1926) and a larger rocket constructed in 1941

Pershing II (U.S.) and SS-20 (USSR) missiles—Two trainers that represent the more than 2,600 nuclear intermediate-range ballistic missiles banned by the 1987 INF Treaty

HIGHLIGHTS—UPPER LEVEL

Wright 1903 Flyer—Wright brothers' aircraft used for the first powered, controlled, and sustained flight by humans in a heavier-than-air craft, 1903

Bell X-1—First piloted flight faster than the speed of sound, 1947

Ryan NYP *Spirit of St. Louis*—Charles Lindbergh's

• TOP: In the Bell X-1 *Glamorous Glennis*, Captain Charles "Chuck" Yeager became the first to achieve supersonic flight, October 14, 1947.

• BOTTOM: *Spirit of St. Louis*, the Ryan NYP (New York to Paris) airplane in which 25-year-old Charles Lindbergh made the first solo nonstop transatlantic flight on May 20 and 21, 1927. The flight took about 33 1/2 hours.

• RIGHT: *Viking* lander, proof-test vehicle for the first U.S. craft to probe the surface of another planet (Mars)

• BELOW: Two French balloonists made the world's first sustained aerial flight in the Montgolfier balloon in 1783 (model).

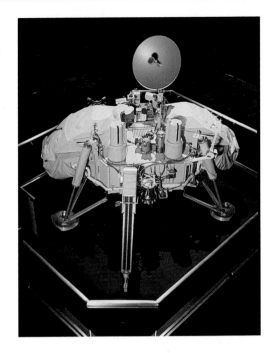

airplane, which made the first solo, nonstop transatlantic flight, 1927

Explorer 1—Backup for the first U.S. satellite to orbit Earth, 1958

Sputnik 1—Soviet replica of the first artificial satellite to orbit Earth, 1957

Pioneer 10—Prototype for the first unmanned spacecraft to fly by Jupiter and Saturn and out of the solar system, launched in 1972

North American X-15—First winged, piloted aircraft to exceed six times the speed of sound (4,534 miles per hour) and the first to explore the fringes of space, 1967

Mariner 2—Backup of the first interplanetary probe to fly by Venus, 1962

Ad Astra—Nickel stainless steel sculpture (1976), by Richard Lippold, at Mall entrance

GALLERY 101—MUSEUM SHOP

GALLERY 102—AIR TRANSPORTATION
Evolution of air transport of people, mail, and cargo

• Among the milestones in aircraft history displayed in the Air Transportation hall are a DC-3, a Ford Tri-motor, a Northrop Alpha, a Fairchild FC-2, and a Boeing 247D.

HIGHLIGHTS

Douglas DC-3—A design milestone and perhaps the single most important aircraft in air transportation history. At 17,500 pounds, the heaviest airplane hanging from the museum's ceiling (1935)

Ford Tri-motor—Offered dependable, safe, and relatively comfortable service when introduced in 1926

Douglas M-2—Operated on the first airmail route between Los Angeles and Salt Lake City, 1926

Pitcairn Mailwing—Efficient, reliable mail carrier, first used in 1927

Northrop Alpha—All-metal, cantilever-wing monoplane, 1930

Fairchild FC-2—Made the first nonstop flight from New York to Miami in 1928

Boeing 247D—First modern airliner, 1933

Douglas DC-7 (nose only)—Visitors can walk through the cockpit of this 1955 airliner.

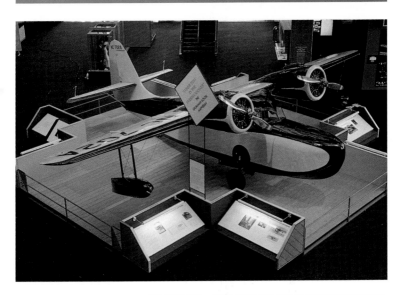

• The Grumman G-21 Amphibian (the "Goose") has been a hard-working hauler of passengers and freight since 1937.

GALLERY 103—DREAM TO FLY: THE BLACK EXPERIENCE IN AVIATION (OPENING 1998–99)

History of African American achievements in the aviation field in the 20th century

GALLERY 104—SPECIAL EXHIBITS

Changing exhibits of aircraft and spacecraft

HIGHLIGHTS

Special exhibits on the history of aeronautics and spaceflight

GALLERY 105—GOLDEN AGE OF FLIGHT

Aviation between the two world wars

HIGHLIGHTS

Beechcraft Staggerwing—Popular general aviation aircraft of the 1930s

Wittman *Buster*—1947 air racer that won the most races in aviation history

Curtiss Robin *Ole Miss*—Set endurance record of 27 days over Meridian, Mississippi, in 1935

Northrop Gamma *Polar Star*—First transantarctic flight, 1935

Hughes H-1—Speed record setter in the 1930s

GALLERY 106—JET AVIATION

The development and present state of jet aviation and its related technology

HIGHLIGHTS

Mural by Keith Ferris—A large-scale depiction of important jet aircraft

Lockheed XP-80—First operational U.S. jet fighter, 1944

Messerschmitt Me 262—First jet fighter in combat, 1942

McDonnell FH-1 Phantom I—First operational carrier-based jet, 1945

Whittle W.1.X—Experimental aircraft engine that powered the British Gloster E.28/39 for taxiing trials in April 1941, becoming unofficially the first British turbojet to be airborne

Heinkel HeS 3B Turbojet—Powered the Heinkel He 178 on the world's first flight of a turbojet-powered aircraft, 1939

Pratt & Whitney JT9D—Huge jet engine used in wide-body jets

Williams WR19—World's smallest turbofan power plant

Films on historic jet aircraft

GALLERY 107—EARLY FLIGHT
The early history of the airplane, from antiquity through the first decade of powered flight

HIGHLIGHTS
Lilienthal glider—The glider that inspired Wilbur and Orville Wright, 1894

Wright Military Flyer—World's first military airplane, 1909

Curtiss Model D "Headless Pusher"—A favorite with U.S. exhibition pilots in the early 1900s

Ecker Flying Boat—Significant pioneering effort in seaplane design, 1912

Blériot XI—Louis Blériot made the first heavier-than-air flight across the English Channel in a similar aircraft on July 25, 1909.

• A Blériot XI, the most popular pre-World War I monoplane, is on view in the Early Flight gallery.

• *Voyager*, the first aircraft to fly around the world nonstop without refueling, is displayed in the South Lobby.

Aeronautical engines—The in-line, radial, and rotary power plants that propelled the first airplanes in the early 1900s

GALLERY 108—INDEPENDENCE AVENUE LOBBY

Aeronautical and astronautical trophies and *Voyager*, flanked by two murals

HIGHLIGHTS

Voyager—First aircraft to fly around the world nonstop without refueling, 1986

Aerospace trophies—Includes names of winners and statements about the trophies' histories

The Space Mural: A Cosmic View—Robert T. McCall's conception of the ancient beginnings of the universe, the triumph of lunar exploration, and an optimistic look into the future

Earthflight Environment—Eric Sloane's dramatic depiction of the remarkable ocean of air that is our atmosphere

Continuum—Bronze sculpture (1976), by Charles O. Perry, outside lobby entrance

GALLERY 109—HOW THINGS FLY

Hands-on exhibits and demonstrations of the scientific principles that allow aircraft and spacecraft to fly

HIGHLIGHTS

Interactive exhibits—More than four dozen hands-on exhibits demonstrating the principles of flight

Cessna 150—Visitors can climb into the cockpit and manipulate the control surfaces

Demonstration stage—Scheduled demonstrations on how things fly and other topics

Resource center—Books, videos, computer programs, and other information

• The Lockheed U-2 has been an important aerial mapping and surveillance craft since the 1950s.

GALLERY 110—LOOKING AT EARTH

Development of technology for viewing Earth from balloons, aircraft, and spacecraft

HIGHLIGHTS

de Havilland DH-4—An American World War I aircraft used extensively for mapping and surveying in the 1920s

Lockheed U-2—Key U.S. reconnaissance aircraft of the Cold War era, with flight suit and typical camera, dating from the late 1950s to the present

Earth observation satellites—Prototype of TIROS, the world's first weather satellite, built in 1960; ITOS weather satellite (engineering test model), 1970s; GOES geostationary satellite (full-scale model), 1975 to the present; and models of other satellites

Landsat image of your state—Interactive touch-screen display showing orbital views of the 50 states

GALLERY 111—STARS

The use of space astronomy satellites to examine the full range of radiant energy from the Sun and stars, unimpeded by Earth's atmosphere

HIGHLIGHTS

Solar instruments—Orbiting Solar Observatory 1, Solrad, Apollo telescope mount

Stellar instruments—Uhuru, International Ultraviolet Explorer, Copernicus, IRAS, Hubble Space Telescope (1-to-5 scale model)

Interactive experiences—Fusion Game, Birthday Star, IUE
Films—*Powers of Ten, Telescopes of Today and Tomorrow, Where the Galaxies Are*

GALLERY 112—LUNAR EXPLORATION VEHICLES
Exploring the Moon

• The lunar roving vehicle allowed astronauts to travel greater distances and carry bulky equipment.

HIGHLIGHTS

Apollo Lunar Module—Duplicate of the spacecraft that carried astronauts to the surface of the Moon in the late 1960s and early 1970s; Apollo space suit replicas
Surveyor—Soft-landed on the Moon to study lunar soil composition and physical properties of the lunar surface, 1966–68
Lunar Orbiter—Circled the Moon and mapped the entire lunar surface, 1966–67
Ranger—Provided the first closeup photographs of the lunar surface, 1962–65

GALLERY 113—ROCKETRY AND SPACEFLIGHT
Science, technology, and the human desire to leave Earth and fly into space, from the 13th century to the present

HIGHLIGHTS

Historical artifacts and models—Representing some of the major contributions in the development of vehicles capable of spaceflight
Rocket engines—Propulsive devices (solid and liquid propellant) that power space boosters and maneuver spacecraft
Space suits—From high-altitude aviators' flight suits to fully independent life-support space suits as used on the Moon

GALLERY 114—SPACE HALL
Space boosters, guided missiles, manned spacecraft, and the space race

HIGHLIGHTS

Skylab orbital workshop—A walk-through backup Skylab spacecraft, the first U.S. space station, 1973–74
Hubble Space Telescope—Full-size test model of observatory put in orbit by Space Shuttle, 1990
Apollo-Soyuz Test Project—First international manned space mission, 1975
Viking—U.S. Navy sounding rocket developed for scientific purposes, 1949–55

Aerobee—Major carrier of scientific instruments for probing the upper atmosphere, 1947–85
V-2—First operational long-range ballistic missile, 1944–45
Jupiter-C and Vanguard boosters—First two U.S. satellite launch vehicles, 1958
Scout-D—Solid-propellant launch vehicle for scientific satellites, 1961–94
Minuteman III—U.S. Air Force intercontinental ballistic missile, 1970 to the present
M2-F3 lifting body—Prepared the way for the development of the Space Shuttle orbiter, 1966–72
Space Shuttle—Model of the shuttle orbiter *Columbia* on its launch pad; shuttle flight clothing and Spacelab model, 1981 to the present

*ABOVE: Visitors may walk through the Skylab orbital workshop, the first U.S. space station.

GALLERY 115—SAMUEL P. LANGLEY THEATER
Films on flight and the environment are shown on a huge screen five stories high and seven stories wide. Spectacular results are achieved with the IMAX projection system. Admission fee.

GALLERY 201—ALBERT EINSTEIN PLANETARIUM
Lectures on the night sky and multimedia programs on astronomy and space are presented in the domed theater. The Zeiss Model VI planetarium projector accurately simulates the nighttime sky and the motions of the sun, Moon, and planets. Admission fee.

*BELOW: *Destiny in Space*, a film presented on the big screen in the Samuel P. Langley Theater, reveals how today's space technology extends our vision to other worlds in the solar system and beyond. Here, astronauts work in orbit 200 miles above Earth.

*OPPOSITE: A view of Space Hall, showing rockets in the missile pit and the Hubble Space Telescope.

GALLERY 203—SEA-AIR OPERATIONS
Aircraft carrier operations from 1911 to the present

HIGHLIGHTS

Carrier hangar deck—Major aircraft from different periods in sea-air history

Boeing F4B-4—Biplane shipboard fighter used from 1932 to 1937

Douglas SBD Dauntless—Principal carrier-based dive bomber used during most of World War II

Grumman FM-1 Wildcat—First-line Navy fighter at the start of World War II

Douglas A-4 Skyhawk—First-line naval attack aircraft of the 1950s and 1960s

Carrier War in the Pacific—The six major aircraft carrier battles in the Pacific during World War II

Modern Carrier Aviation—Developments in carrier construction, operations, roles, and missions in the nuclear age

GALLERY 205—WORLD WAR II AVIATION
Fighter aircraft from five countries

HIGHLIGHTS

North American P-51D Mustang—An outstanding fighter airplane, used in every theater of the war

Mitsubishi A6M5 Zero—With excellent maneuverability and range, used in almost every action throughout the war by the Japanese navy

Martin B-26 *Flak Bait* (nose only)—Flew the most missions of any American bomber in Europe

• The Sea-Air Operations gallery features a replica of the hangar deck of an aircraft carrier.

• TOP: The North American P-51 Mustang was one of the best fighter airplanes to see action in World War II.

• MIDDLE: Japan's Mitsubishi A6M5 Zero was noted for its maneuverability and speed.

• BOTTOM: The Albatros D.Va (above) and the Royal Aircraft Factory F.E.8 displayed in the Legend, Memory, and the Great War in the Air gallery

Supermarine Spitfire Mark VII—A later version of the legendary British fighter that helped defeat the Germans in the Battle of Britain

Messerschmitt Bf 109G—Principal Luftwaffe fighter and the major opponent of Spitfires and American bombers

Macchi C.202 Folgore—Most successful Italian fighter to see extensive service. Used in the African campaign and in Italy and the Soviet Union

GALLERY 206—LEGEND, MEMORY, AND THE GREAT WAR IN THE AIR

The emergence of air power in World War I

HIGHLIGHTS

Voisin 8—Early type of night bomber, 1915

SPAD XIII—French fighter aircraft also used by Americans

Fokker D.VII—Considered the best German fighter aircraft of World War I

Albatros D.Va—German fighter aircraft that flew on all fronts during World War I

Sopwith Snipe—British aircraft considered one of the best all-around single-seat fighters, although it came quite late in the war

German factory scene—World War I mass-production techniques, with original equipment

GALLERY 207—EXPLORING THE PLANETS

History and achievements of planetary exploration, both Earth-based and by spacecraft

HIGHLIGHTS

Voyager—Full-scale replica of the spacecraft that explored Jupiter, Saturn, Uranus, and Neptune in the 1970s and 1980s

The *Viking* View of Mars—Backup spacecraft equipment for the *Viking* landers; video, *Mars: The Movie*

A Piece of Mars?—Meteorite collected in Antarctica that may have come from Mars

***Surveyor 3* television camera**—Retrieved from the surface of the Moon by the Apollo 12 astronauts

GALLERY 208—PIONEERS OF FLIGHT

Famous "firsts" and record setters

HIGHLIGHTS

Lockheed Sirius *Tingmissartoq*—Flown by Charles and Anne Lindbergh on airline-route mapping flights, 1930s

Amelia Earhart's transatlantic Lockheed Vega—First solo flight across the Atlantic by a woman, 1932

Fokker T-2—First nonstop U.S. transcontinental flight, 1923

Gossamer Condor—First successful human-powered aircraft

Douglas World Cruiser *Chicago*—First around-the-world flight, 1924

***Explorer II* gondola**—This cabin and its balloon rose to a height never before achieved and made valuable scientific observations, 1935.

Montgolfier balloon (model)—First aerial vehicle to carry human beings aloft, 1783

•ABOVE: In 1932, Amelia Earhart became the first woman to make a solo transatlantic flight. She flew this Lockheed Vega from Newfoundland to Northern Ireland in 14 hours, 52 minutes.

•RIGHT: Central to the Where Next, Columbus? gallery is a realistic Martian landscape featuring robotic and human explorers.

Black Wings: The American Black in Aviation—Chronicles the struggle of African Americans to earn a place in aeronautics and spaceflight in the United States
Changing exhibits—Honoring aviation personalities

GALLERY 209—WHERE NEXT, COLUMBUS?
Challenges and choices for future explorers

HIGHLIGHTS
Mars terrain—A realistic landscape of our neighbor world
Space garden—Fresh food for space explorers
Stellarium—A fiber-optic map of our neighborhood in the Milky Way
Interactive experiences—Send a Robot to Mars, Join a Human Mission to Mars, Visitor Opinion Poll
Films—*Other Worlds, Spacefaring, Contact!*

GALLERY 210—APOLLO TO THE MOON
Triumph of manned spaceflight in the 1960s and early 1970s, from Project Mercury through the Apollo Moon landings

HIGHLIGHTS
F-1 engine—Full-size, with cutaway of first-stage engine used on Saturn V rocket
Astronautical items and equipment—Used during the Apollo missions
Lunar scenes—Showing the Lunar Rover and astronauts at work on the Moon
Saturn boosters—Models of Saturn IB and Saturn V rockets
Lunar samples—Four types of lunar soil and rocks
Space food—How astronauts' and cosmonauts' food has changed
Space suits—Worn by Apollo astronauts on the Moon

• Five F-1 rocket engines were needed to lift the huge Saturn V vehicle from its launch pad.

GALLERY 211—FLIGHT AND THE ARTS
Works of art, popular culture, and films relating to the theme of aeronautics and spaceflight

HIGHLIGHTS
Changing exhibitions of art, literature, television, film, and popular culture artifacts from public and private collections

GALLERY 213—BEYOND THE LIMITS: FLIGHT ENTERS THE COMPUTER AGE
How computers are used in aerospace design and operations

• TOP: The HiMAT remotely piloted experimental aircraft, featured in the gallery Beyond the Limits: Flight Enters the Computer Age

• BOTTOM: A full-scale model of the innovative X-29 hangs in the Beyond the Limits gallery.

X-29—Forward-swept-wing airplane (full-scale model)

Cray-1 supercomputer—World's fastest computer

Interactive computers—Visitors can try out computer-aided design, flight simulation, airline scheduling, and flight testing

Space Station Theater—Films on flight simulation, the X-29, and computer software

HiMAT—Robot airplane that pioneered the use of fly-by-wire technology, in which a computer—not the pilot—controls the aircraft's flaps, rudder, and ailerons

Minuteman III ICBM Guidance and Control System—The brain of the Minuteman missile, the standard U.S. land-based intercontinental ballistic missile

PAUL E. GARBER FACILITY

HIGHLIGHTS

Lockheed P-38J Lightning, Hawker Hurricane, and Focke-Wulf Fw 190—Just a few of the famous World War II fighter planes on display

Roscoe Turner's RT-14 *Meteor*—A racer from the golden age of aviation

Curtiss JN-4D Jenny—An aircraft made famous by the barnstormers after World War I

North American F-86A and MiG-15—Arch rivals in the Korean War

The Paul E. Garber Preservation, Restoration, and Storage Facility in Suitland, Maryland, houses the National Air and Space Museum's reserve collection of historically significant airplanes and spacecraft.

Used since the mid-1950s as a storage and restoration center, the facility now has several buildings open to the public as a "no-frills" museum. Exhibited here are more than 150 aircraft, as well as many spacecraft, engines, propellers, and other flight-related objects. Guided tours include a behind-the-scenes look at the workshop where all phases of the restoration process are handled—from upholstery repair to engine reconstruction.

The facility is named for the late Paul E. Garber, historian emeritus and Ramsey Fellow of the National Air and Space Museum, who joined the Smithsonian Institution in 1920 and was responsible for acquiring a large portion of the aeronautical collection.

• The restoration staff at the Paul E. Garber Preservation, Restoration, and Storage Facility after restoring the Voisin VIII French bomber, originally built in about 1918.

• TOP: Craftsmen at the Paul E. Garber Facility restoring a 1914 Blériot XI monoplane.

• BOTTOM: Three hangar-like buildings are open to the public at the Paul E. Garber Facility. A yellow World War II Stearman trainer can be seen on the left.

TOURS

Free tours are available Monday through Friday at 10 a.m. and Saturday and Sunday at 10 a.m. and 1 p.m. Reservations must be made at least two weeks in advance. Call (202) 357-1400 or TTY (202) 357-1505 between 9 a.m. and 3:15 p.m., Monday through Friday, or write to: Educational Services Department, Reservations Office, MRC 305, National Air and Space Museum, Washington, D.C. 20560.

Individuals or groups of up to 40 may take the guided tours, which last about three hours. Special tours for disabled visitors are available on request.

NOTE: There is no heating or air conditioning in the warehouse-type exhibit areas.

NATIONAL MUSEUM OF NATURAL HISTORY/

NATIONAL MUSEUM OF MAN

Constitution Avenue (accessible entrance) at 10th Street, NW

Mall entrance: Madison Drive

between 9th and 12th Streets, NW

Open daily except December 25, 10 a.m. to 5:30 p.m.

(Extended spring and summer hours determined annually)

Metro station: Federal Triangle

Smithsonian information: (202) 357-2700

Information recording in Spanish: (202) 633-9126

TTY: (202) 357-1729 (for callers with communication impairments)

The National Museum of Natural History/National Museum of Man is dedicated to understanding the natural world and the place of humans in it. As the nation's largest research museum, it is a treasure house of more than 121 million specimens of plants, animals, rocks, gems and minerals, fossils, and human cultural artifacts. This encyclopedic collection is an essential resource for

NATIONAL MUSEUM OF NATURAL HISTORY/
NATIONAL MUSEUM OF MAN

GROUND FLOOR

1   Museum Shop (opens 6/96)
2   Restaurant (opens 7/98)
3   The Court Restaurant (until 5/96)
4   Baird Auditorium
5-6 Birds of Washington, D.C.

FIRST FLOOR

7   Butterfly Garden (outside, along 9th Street)
8   Rotunda (including African Bush Elephant)
9   Dinosaurs
10   Early Life
11   Fossil Plants
12   Fossil Mammals
13   Ancient Seas
14   Ice Age
15   Special Exhibitions (through 1996); Cultures of Africa (opens 1997)
16   Cultures of Asia
17   Cultures of the Pacific
18   Special Exhibitions
19-20 Native Cultures of the Americas
21   Discovery Room (until 7/98)
22   North American Mammals
23   Birds of the World
24-25 World of Mammals
26   Exploring Marine Ecosystems
27   Blue Whale
28   In Search of Giant Squid
29   Museum Shop (until 5/96)
30   Cafeteria (until 6/96)
31   Discovery Center (opens 7/98)

SECOND FLOOR

32   Hope diamond (until 12/96)
33   Janet Annenberg Hooker Hall of Geology, Gems and Minerals (opens 12/96)
34   Harry Winston Gallery (Hope diamond after 12/96)
35   National Gem Collection
36   Minerals and Crystals
37   Mine re-creation
38   Rocks Gallery
39   Plate Tectonics Gallery
40   Earth, Moon, and Meteorites
41   Museum Shop (gems and minerals)
42   South America: Continent and Culture
43   Origins of Western Culture
44   Bones
45   Reptiles
46   O. Orkin Insect Zoo

Constitution Avenue entrance

To accessible entrance

Mall entrance

Legend:
? Information
⚲ Checkroom
✚ First Aid
Guard Office
|||| Stairs
Escalators
⊠ Elevators
Restrooms
Accessible Entrance
Telephone
$ Automated Teller Machine

AT A GLANCE

Dinosaurs, the Hope diamond, the African bush elephant, Native American objects, Exploring Marine Ecosystems, and the O. Orkin Insect Zoo are among the most popular features of this museum.

Also of special interest is the Discovery Room, where visitors of all ages can touch, feel, smell, and taste a variety of natural specimens, and the exhibition Life in the Ancient Seas.

• The museum is undergoing extensive renovation in preparation for the opening of its exciting new Discovery Center in 1998. Construction schedules are subject to change, so please inquire at a museum information desk for the most up-to-date floor plan.

INFORMATION DESKS

Near the Mall and Constitution Avenue entrances

TOURS

Guided public walk-in tours are given daily at 10:30 a.m. and 1:30 p.m., September through June. Confirm tour times at information desks or call (202) 357-2700; TTY (202) 357-1729. The museum offers lesson tours for school groups during the academic year. Request school tours in writing well ahead of planned visits. For an application form, call (202) 357-2747 or TTY (202) 633-9287. Self-guided audio tours are available in the rotunda on the first floor.

ACCESS

The Mall entrance is not accessible to visitors in wheelchairs and those who cannot climb stairs readily. Most museum services are accessible to visitors with disabilities. Loop amplifications are available in the center front rows of Baird Auditorium. For special services for groups, call (202) 786-2178, fax (202) 786-2778, or TTY (202) 633-9287. To receive a large-type version of the text of *Quest*, a free quarterly newsletter that includes the museum's calendar of events, call (202) 357-4014 or TTY (202) 633-9287.

WHERE TO EAT

The public cafeteria on the first floor currently offers hamburgers, submarine sandwiches, salads, desserts, beverages, and other lunch items in a casual atmosphere. In The Court restaurant on the ground floor, guests can enjoy an extensive salad bar, luncheon buffet, and gourmet desserts.

NOTE: All museum restaurant facilities will close in June 1996 during construction of the museum's new Discovery Center, which will open in 1998.

MUSEUM SHOP

The main museum shop carries a variety of Smithsonian souvenirs and natural history–related gifts, including a wide selection of jewelry, books, cassette tapes, and compact discs. An adjacent shop is especially appealing to children, and several theme-oriented shops elsewhere in the museum feature books and memorabilia relating to permanent and special exhibitions.

NOTE: The main museum shop will close in May 1996 during the construction of the new Discovery Center. It will reopen on the ground floor in June 1996.

DISCOVERY ROOM

This special area on the first floor is a family-oriented, flexible education facility featuring multisensory experiences with objects from the world of nature. Hours are Monday through Thursday, noon to 2:30 p.m.; Friday, Saturday, and Sunday, 10:30 a.m. to 3:30 p.m. Free passes are distributed daily at the room entrance. Groups of more than five are not admitted during regular hours. One adult must accompany every two to three children. For a group reservation application form, call (202) 357-2747, fax (202) 786-2778, or TTY (202) 633-9287.

NOTE: The Discovery Room will move to the museum's new Discovery Center in 1998 or later.

DISCOVERY CENTER

Opening in 1998, the Discovery Center will offer visitors a state-of-the-art large-format theater, an updated restaurant, a consolidated museum shop, and an enhanced Discovery Room. The Samuel C. Johnson Theater will show three-dimensional films on a screen 20 meters (66 feet) high and 27 meters (90 feet) wide. There will be seating for about 400 viewers. An enlarged restaurant will serve a variety of meal, snack, and refreshment items. The new museum shop will be more than twice as large as the existing shops. It will include a children's area, bookstore, and ethnic-craft section. The new Discovery Room will be located on the top level.

scientists studying the earth sciences, the biological world, and human origins and cultures. Exhibitions and educational programs attract large numbers of visitors every year to the museum's green-domed Beaux Arts building, one of Washington's best-known landmarks.

Only a tiny portion of the collection is on public display. Many of the objects are housed in the Smithsonian's Museum Support Center in Suitland, Maryland, which provides state-of-the-art conditions for the storage and conservation of research collections. Behind the scenes in the laboratories and offices at the museum and the support center, more than 100 scholars conduct research in association with colleagues from universities, other museums, and government agencies.

The story told in these halls is the story of our planet from its wild, fiery beginnings to its transformation over the next 3.5 billion years by a marvelous web of evolving life, including our own species. Living and nonliving, art and artifact: Taken together, they reveal a wondrous and complex world.

GROUND FLOOR

Just inside the Constitution Avenue entrance is an exhibit that introduces the wonders of the museum. Among the 250 highlights are amethysts and pyrite crystals, a 700,000-year-old hand ax from Kenya, pottery by the renowned Pueblo artists

●LEFT: The eight-sided rotunda is ringed with colorful banners marking some of the hall entrances.

●RIGHT: Magnificent Haida and Tsimshian carved cedar totem poles, collected in the Pacific Northwest more than 100 years ago, soar into the North Lobby stairwell. In terms of aesthetic quality and condition, these are among the best totem poles in existence.

DISCOVERY ROOM

• In the Discovery Room visitors of all ages can use their senses to explore objects from the museum's anthropological, biological, geological, and paleontological collections.

Maria Martinez and Nampeo, totem poles from the Northwest Coast, a gigantic tooth from a fossil shark, meteorites, a calcite-encrusted bird's nest, and morpho butterflies from South America.

Baird Auditorium, used for lectures, concerts, films, and other special events, is located on the ground floor. Outside the auditorium is Baird Gallery, where almost 300 mounted species of birds of the eastern United States are on display. They include some superb examples of hawks and eagles. (For the location of the museum's Birds of the World exhibit on the first floor, ask at an information desk or consult the map in this guide.)

FIRST FLOOR

THE ROTUNDA

Entered from the National Mall, the eight-sided rotunda is one of Washington, D.C.'s splendid spaces. It is 38 meters (125 feet) high from the marble floor to the tiled dome. The first-story columns are Doric in style, and the second- and third-story columns are Roman and Ionic. Many of the architectural details are best seen from the second-floor rotunda balcony.

An African bush elephant, one of the largest and most powerful land animals in the world, stands in

• A mosasaur nabs an ammonite. Like the dinosaurs, mosasaurs and other gigantic marine reptiles died out 65 million years ago.

• Modern humans are shown at the top of this "tower of time" as part of the ever-changing sequence of life on Earth.

the rotunda. This spectacular elephant weighed about 8 tons and stood 4 meters (13 feet 2 inches) tall at the shoulder.

FOSSILS: THE HISTORY OF LIFE

This major exhibition presents highlights from the beginnings of life in the sea 3.5 billion years ago.

Earliest Traces of Life includes the oldest fossil, a cabbage-sized 3.5-billion-year-old mass built by microorganisms. An animated film and a dramatic mural trace the origin and the evolution of life, while a time column standing more than 8 meters (27 feet) high shows an index of geologic time.

A Grand Opening: Fossils Galore documents the dramatic explosion of hard-shelled life at the beginning of the Paleozoic Era 570 million years ago. Rare 530-million-year-old fossilized soft-bodied animals of the Burgess Shale are on display here. These fossils, which are among the Smithsonian's greatest finds, were discovered in 1910 by the Institution's fourth secretary, geologist Charles D. Walcott.

Life in the Ancient Seas showcases prehistoric marine life, emphasizing evolutionary innovations and describing the existence of these unfamiliar animals and plants. Through sound and lighting, the hall gives the feeling of being underwater in the marine realm. Among the approximately 2,000 fossils on exhibit are the 14-meter-(45-foot-) long skeleton of *Basilosaurus* (an early whale) and a spectacular slab of sea lilies from the early Carboniferous period 345 to 325 million years ago. To bring these creatures to life, the exhibition features a series of murals showing the fleshed-out animals these fossils once were and a full-scale diorama of a 250-million-year-old reef made of more than 100,000 models.

The Conquest of Land focuses on the earliest plants and animals to evolve the complex adaptations needed to live on land. In an animated video

• This mural in "Earliest Traces of Life" depicts life on the primitive Earth approximately 3.5 billion years ago. Scientists envision the planet at that time—when the earliest known life began to appear—as volcanically active, with rapid erosion on the barren terrain.

• TOP: A life-sized model of a pterosaur with a 40-foot wingspan soars above visitors. This flying reptile was twice as large as any bird that ever lived.

• MIDDLE: In this reconstruction of a Neandertal burial in France about 70,000 years ago, the body of a young man was carefully placed on a bear skin in a stone-lined pit. Offerings of bear meat and stone tools were then placed on a slab above the body and covered with rocks. A funeral fire was lit on top.

• BOTTOM: The woolly mammoth—an extinct elephant species that once abounded in North America and northern Eurasia—reached enormous size during the Ice Age. This skeleton is on display in the Ice Age hall.

evoking television coverage of the first lunar landing, characters Frank Anchorfish and Arthur Pod explain what plants and animals needed to pioneer the harsh, dry terrestrial environment. Just beyond an arbor formed by a diorama of the first forests are still more fossils: specimens of a 9-meter (16-foot) fossil of an early tree, *Callixylon*; other fossil trees and smaller plants from the ancient coal forests of North America; and skeletons of many amphibians. Completing the section are displays on the seed and the amniotic egg—the two evolutionary innovations that secured the conquest of land for plants and animals.

Flowering Plants displays fossils of many early ancestors of today's vegetation and includes slabs of petrified wood in a sunlit lounge.

•RIGHT: Only 14,000 years ago, this saber-toothed cat became mired in the tar pits of Rancho La Brea, California.

•BELOW: The 80-foot-long skeleton of *Diplodocus* dominates the dinosaur hall. A member of the sauropod family, it was the largest animal ever to have walked the earth.

Reptiles—Masters of Land features the skeletons of dinosaurs, the great reptiles that dominated Earth for 140 million years until their extinction about 65 million years ago. *Diplodocus*, a 24-meter- (80-foot-) long member of the sauropod family of dinosaurs, the largest land-dwelling animals of all time, towers over skeletons of *Camptosaurus*, *Stegosaurus*, and *Allosaurus*, a fearsome predator.

Mammals in the Limelight focuses on the spectacular explosion of mammalian evolution following the extinction of dinosaurs. Four huge murals re-create scenes of animal and plant life in succes-

sive epochs of the Age of Mammals. The murals provide settings for fossil specimens, including mounted skeletons, many of them assembled from fossils unearthed in the American West by Smithsonian scientists. The different stages of horse evolution are shown in fossil specimens, an animated film, and a mural.

ICE AGE MAMMALS AND THE EMERGENCE OF MAN

The Ice Age was one of the most extraordinary periods in Earth's history. At the entrance to this exhibition, a cast of a 24,800-year-old mammoth tusk, beautifully engraved by an early artist, symbolizes the emergence of humans as a dominant influence on the environment. Mounted skeletons of some of the largest Ice Age mammals dominate the hall: a giant ground sloth, a woolly mammoth, and an Irish elk. Also on exhibit is an Ice Age bison, freeze-dried by nature and recovered by gold miners in Alaska. A life-sized tableau of a Neandertal burial shows that at least 70,000 years ago our ancestors carefully buried their dead and may have believed in an afterlife.

ASIAN AND PACIFIC CULTURES

Crafts and objects from the daily life of peoples from Asia, India, and the Pacific are seen in this exhibition. Everyday objects form a central display about the various nationalities of Asia. A diorama presents a scene from a Chinese opera. There are also Shinto and Confucian shrines and an iron Buddha from Korea. Other exhibits tell about Asian music, calligraphy, and language; the music and crafts of Thailand, India, and Pakistan; and the shadow puppets of Malaysia. Objects of daily life from China and the Ryukyu Islands are shown along with a room from a Korean house. The ancient Cambodian Khmer culture is featured, as is the imposing figure of a Fijian high chief wearing ceremonial black-and-white painted bark cloth.

In the Pacific Islands areas are exhibits devoted to the Native peoples of Indonesia, Melanesia, Polynesia, Micronesia, Australia, New Zealand, and the Philippines. Among them are a diorama showing tattooing as practiced by the Maoris of New Zealand and two huge stone discs used as money on Yap in the Caroline Islands. Other displays feature boomerangs and bark painting by aborigines of Arnhem Land, sailing and fishing in Polynesia, and rice growing in the Philippines. One of the famous massive stone heads from Easter Island stands at the rotunda entrance to the hall.

AFRICAN HISTORY AND CULTURES
(OPENING IN 1997)

Africa's most striking characteristics are its immense size and wide variety of peoples. More than three times the size of the continental United States, Africa today is home to more than 300 million people inhabiting more than 50 countries. The African continent is divided by the boundaries of its na-

• OPPOSITE: A stone head from Easter Island in the South Pacific.

• RIGHT: One of the largest "coins" ever used—a stone disc from the Micronesian island of Yap.

• BELOW: Bronze heads have been cast to memorialize the rulers of the Benin Kingdom in present-day Nigeria from the 14th century to the present. This sculpture dates to the 16th or 17th century.

tion-states as well as by diverse language groups, cultures, ecological zones, and histories.

This new exhibition will resonate with the dynamism of contemporary African culture. It will examine the overlapping, continuously broadening spheres of African influence—historical and contemporary, local and international—in the realms of family, work, commerce, and the natural environment. Objects such as a 17th-century cast brass head from the Benin Kingdom of Nigeria, a late-19th-century carved wooden staff by the Luba of Zaire, and decorative fiber headwear from 19th- and 20th-century Zaire will show the aesthetic dimensions of leadership in certain African societies. A late-19th-century copper-and-brass image made by the Kota peoples of Gabon and a contemporary Afro-Cuban altar will demonstrate the enduring presence of African belief systems on the African continent and in Africa's diaspora. Akan gold weights, Ethiopian silver crosses, and decorated ceramic vessels will explore the history of metallurgy and pottery in diverse regions of Africa. Objects used in everyday life, contemporary fashion, children's toys, musical instruments, and excerpts from oral poetry, song, and literary texts will illustrate the transatlantic connection between Africa and the Americas.

ESKIMO AND INDIAN CULTURES

This hall is arranged according to cultural areas—regions in which Native American cultures are broadly similar through shared histories and adaptations to similar environments. Near the rotunda, several dioramas depict the adaptations of northern peoples to harsh Arctic conditions. Displays on seal hunting, ice fishing, and igloo construction lead to an exhibit of Eskimo art. Following the section on the Arctic region is the Eastern Woodland culture section where a birch-bark canoe, lacrosse sticks, and other objects are displayed. In the Plains Indians exhibit there is a tipi made of 14 buffalo hides and decorated with porcupine quills. The tipi was obtained for the 1876 Centennial Exposition in Philadelphia, just at the end of the buffalo-hunting era.

At the far end of this hall is a collection of Northwest Coast art objects, including a superb display of masks. Exhibits on Native American culture are produced by the museum in association with Native people. Seminole Interpretations presents traditional and contemporary aspects of life among this Florida tribe today. A display of baskets made by tribal masters from all over the country is on view. In a five-minute video, Mary

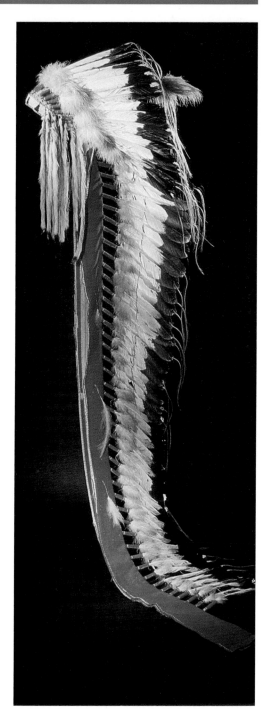

•OPPOSITE TOP: Navajo silversmiths (ca. 1880) melted coins, cast basic shapes in stone or metal molds, and then hammered and decorated the pieces by hand.

•OPPOSITE MIDDLE: The recently added Seminole Interpretations display shows how members of this Florida tribe have incorporated their cultural traditions into contemporary life.

•OPPOSITE BOTTOM: Birds of the Antarctic include Emperor and Adelie penguins.

•RIGHT: This Sioux chief's eagle feather bonnet (ca. 1880) includes 77 eagle feathers along with beadwork, trade cloth, and white weasel skin.

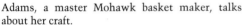

Adams, a master Mohawk basket maker, talks about her craft.

Other exhibits portray Native American cultures of California, the southwestern United States, Mexico, Guatemala, the Andean region, Panama, the West Indies, the South American tropical forest, Patagonia, and Tierra del Fuego. Short films about today's Native American peoples are also shown.

BIRDS

Specimens from all over the world are displayed here in realistic poses, with their differences in form, size, and color emphasized. The exhibition illustrates migration, reproduction, feeding habits, flight, and birds' importance to people. Birds of special interest are shown in their natural habitats: the appealing Antarctic penguins, the ostrich with babies just hatched from their eggs, and the argus pheasant, noted for its enormous plumes. Some of the birds were once abundant in North America but were driven to extinction by the human hand. They include the penguinlike great auk, the Carolina parakeet, and the passenger pigeon. Though numerous as recently as the 19th century, not a single passenger pigeon remains alive today; the last died in captivity in 1914.

• ABOVE LEFT: Passenger pigeons, once America's most abundant bird, were extinct in the wild by 1900. "Martha," the last survivor, died in captivity in 1914.

• ABOVE RIGHT: The museum's Exploring Marine Ecosystems exhibit includes two model ecosystems, one simulating a Caribbean coral reef (above), and the other replicating the rocky coast of Maine.

SEA LIFE: EXPLORING MARINE ECOSYSTEMS

On our ocean planet, scientists are constantly discovering new features of marine communities. At the rotunda entrance to this hall is a simulated Maine kelp forest, 9 meters (30 feet) deep, complete with kelp plants, sea stars, lobsters, and other organisms that make up the food web in this marine ecosystem. Ahead are two model ecosystems that simulate a tropical coral reef of the Caribbean and natural conditions on Maine's rocky coast. The colorful inhabitants of the reef tank include living corals; tangs; parrot fish; crabs; and blue-green, green, and red algae. In contrast, the cold-water tank contains kelp, rockweed, marsh grass, lobsters, scallops, mussels, hake, and tomcod. Scientists are

• Life-sized illustrations on this banner show visitors to "In Search of Giant Squid" how large these animals can get.

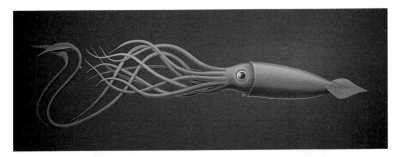

using these ecosystems, which are based on more than 25 years of field and laboratory research by a Smithsonian scientist, to seek a better understanding of how natural ocean communities function.

Suspended above the Sea Life hall is a model of a huge blue whale, 28 meters (92 feet) long. Now endangered, blue whales are the largest mammals living today. Below the whale is information on blue whale biology, migration routes, historic population numbers, and photographs of the whales in their natural habitat.

In Search of Giant Squid, an exhibition in the rear of the Sea Life hall, explores and interprets the mystery, beauty, and complexity of giant squid, the world's largest invertebrates. Two giant squid, the only ones on view in a museum in the world, are displayed in clear acrylic tanks. The 2-meter (7-foot), 61-kilogram (135-pound) bioluminescent *Taningia danae* is among the largest of its kind on record. Large adults of this species are rarely captured, and fewer than a dozen have been documented. Scientists have never seen this species alive in its natural habitat. On its eight long arms are sharp hooks to grasp its prey. At the tips of two of the arms are strobe-flash organs, or photophores, which flash a brilliant blue-green light, startling predators and al-

lowing the squid to make a quick getaway. *Taningia* lives between the ocean's surface and a depth of nearly one kilometer (3,238 feet), feeding mainly on fishes and other squid. Its eyes, the largest in the animal kingdom, are the size of grapefruits, and its head houses a complex brain. A five-minute video shows Smithsonian scientists in the field studying giant squid in collaboration with other researchers.

Two other remarkable sea animals, the walrus and the sea otter, are on center stage at the rear of the Sea Life hall. An imposing mounted specimen of a walrus is on view, and a film about pinnipeds describes this family of mammals that also includes the seal and sea lion. A sea otter is also highlighted. The sea otter's diet consists mainly of hard-shelled prey, which the animals pound against flat rocks to break and open the shell. Except for humans and a few other primates, the otter is unique in its use of a tool.

THE WORLD OF MAMMALS

Exhibited in these halls in life settings are hundreds of fascinating mammals. Mammals are warm-blooded, have backbones, have hair at some time in life, and nourish their young with milk. This exhibition explains the classification of mammals, their adaptations to various environments, and the relationships of nonhuman mammals to humans.

The Tiger! display captures the explosive moment when a Bengal tiger leaps after its prey, an axis deer. Despite aggressive conservation measures, the number of tigers in their diminishing habitat along the India-Nepal border declined in just 20 years from 40,000 to fewer than 2,000.

• **ABOVE:** Mountain goats forage on sparse vegetation in the Rockies in this life-like scene in the Mammals hall.

• **OPPOSITE TOP:** The 45.5-carat Hope diamond is the best-known and largest deep blue diamond in the world.

• **OPPOSITE BOTTOM:** The emeralds in the Inquisition Necklace are some of the most perfect on display anywhere in the world.

SECOND FLOOR

This new hall, located off the second-floor rotunda balcony, will be the world's most comprehensive

earth science complex. The legendary Hope diamond—a must for every museum visitor—will be on view here in the Harry Winston Gallery. (It can now be seen in a temporary vault on the second floor.) The 45.5-carat blue diamond was named for Henry Philip Hope of England, who once owned it. Evalyn Walsh McLean of Washington, D.C., was the last private owner, and the diamond is still in the setting made for her. Acquired from her estate in 1949 by the New York jewelry firm of Harry Winston, Inc., the rare and magnificent gem was given to the Smithsonian by Harry Winston in 1958.

Spectacular examples of other geological objects will also be displayed in the Harry Winston Gallery: huge quartz crystals from Africa; one of the largest sheets of naturally formed, nearly pure copper in existence; a natural sandstone "sculpture"; polished gneiss formed deep within the earth; and a ring-shaped meteorite from outer space.

The National Gem Collection Gallery in the new hall will include the Marie Antoinette earrings (one of the last gifts from King Louis XVI to his queen), the 127-carat Portuguese diamond, the Rosser Reeves ruby with its unparalleled six-rayed star, and the Hooker starburst diamonds, among the most perfect of their kind.

Other highlights of the Janet Annenberg Hooker Hall will be a gallery displaying some 2,500 of the most spectacular crystals and minerals from the National Mineral Collections. A simulated mine will show how crystal pockets, ore veins, and other rocks and minerals formed within the earth. How rocks have been built, bent, broken, and baked in ages past is the subject of the Rocks Gallery. Plate tectonics will be explained in a display and theater that show how the heat of Earth's interior drives the movement of the vast plates that form its outermost layer. Earthquakes and volcanoes are among the most visible results of this plate movement, and the exhibit will highlight museum volcanologists' contributions to our understanding of these processes. Also featured will be an exhibit about differences in the development of Earth and the Moon, complete with Moon rocks and interstellar dust.

SOUTH AMERICA: CONTINENT AND CULTURE

This hall shows the distinctive environments and resources of four South American regions and the different ways in which cultures have adapted to them during the Prehistoric, Colonial, and Modern

● TOP: The 138-carat Rosser Reeves ruby is probably the largest fine star ruby in the world. The fabulous gem was mined in Sri Lanka and donated to the museum in 1965.

● MIDDLE: This specimen of leaf gold, one of the finest of its kind, weighs 454.7 grams (14.6 troy ounces) and comes from the Eureka Mine, California.

● LEFT: A Moon rock collected by Apollo astronauts.

• ABOVE: The unusual Tucson Ring meteorite was claimed in present-day Arizona by a U.S. Army officer, who donated it to the Smithsonian in 1863. It weighs 560 kilograms (1,500 pounds) and measures 90 centimeters by 120 centimeters (3 feet by 4 feet).

• BELOW: This diorama depicts the plaza of a modern Andean town on market day.

eras. A mural and diorama show the first region—the great Patagonian grasslands—as they looked in the 19th century. A hunt is in progress: nomadic Tehuelche Indians armed with bolas ride across the plains in pursuit of fleeing rhea birds. A display of the great trunks, branches, and vines of a lifelike tropical rainforest introduces the next region—the tropics. Despite its lush vegetation, this region supports only marginal agriculture, and the tribes that live in the forest depend on wild foods. The weapons, brightly colored ornaments, and everyday tools of one of the tribes, the Waiwai, are exhibited. Along the arid Pacific coastlands, the third region, fishing and irrigation of farmland helped support large prehistoric populations. A diorama features a balsa raft of the kind coastal people used for thousands of years. The culture of the fourth region—

• ABOVE: Tehuelche Indians, nomadic hunters of the South American grasslands, pursue flightless rheas.

• RIGHT: The early groups of hunter-gatherers who inhabited Lascaux Cave, France, 30,000 years ago left these cave paintings.

• OPPOSITE: Coffins of Tenet-Khonsu, high priestess of the god Amon-Ra, Egypt, about 1000 B.C.

the high Andean mountain valleys—is sustained by abundant potato and corn crops. This region is vividly portrayed in a three-dimensional re-creation of a town plaza featuring a marketplace and church

facade. Objects from the Inca civilization are exhibited beneath a mural of a mountain citadel.

ORIGINS OF WESTERN CULTURE

This exhibit traces the increasing complexity of Western civilization from the end of the Ice Age, about 10,000 years ago, to about A.D. 500. Ice Age flint tools, such as knives and projectile points, and a reconstructed cave with paintings of animals illustrate human dependence on hunting.

After the Ice Age, people in southwestern Asia began the shift to farming as a way of life. A diorama re-creates a scene from Ali Kosh, one of the earliest farming villages. Technological advances accompanied the spread of agriculture. Egyptian pottery from 4,000 B.C. is shown along with increasingly sophisticated stone and bone tools from Europe. Another diorama shows the Mesopotamian city of Larsa in 1801 B.C.

The growing complexity of urban life fostered a new form of political and social organization called

the state, which eventually led to the formation of empires. The complexity of ancient societies is reflected in their burial customs, illustrated in a display of the Bronze Age tombs of Bab-edh-Dhra in Jordan. *City of the Dead*, a video about Smithsonian investigations of the Bronze Age tombs, is shown in the Gilgamesh Theater.

An Egyptian mummy in a coffin in the original wrappings with decorations—surrounded by typical grave goods such as amulets, jewelry, offerings of food, and statues of deities—will go on permanent view in the hall in mid-1996. Videos on ancient Egyptian daily life, arts, tombs, and mummies will be shown.

The growth of empires is illustrated with an outstanding collection of artifacts, including pottery and stone tools from Troy, Luristan bronzes, a Cycladic figurine, Etruscan bronzes, Greek pottery, Roman glass, a Roman mosaic, and Roman money.

By about A.D. 500, the basic patterns of Western culture were set, and many of them persist today. A section of the hall focuses on today with a reconstructed modern bazaar scene. A Roman cookbook is compared with a modern one.

BONES

Hundreds of skeletons of mammals, birds, reptiles, amphibians, and fishes, ranging from the gigantic extinct Steller sea cow to the tiny pocket mouse, are shown in characteristic poses and grouped by order to illustrate their relationships. Exhibits show how bone structures evolved in adaptation to environment. Horses, for example, developed leg and foot bones that enabled them to run swiftly on the level grasslands where they lived and grazed. The skeleton of a famous race horse, Lexington (1850–75), illustrates this adaptation.

REPTILES

The subtropical Florida Everglades—home of alligators, tree frogs, turtles, and a variety of snakes, including the diamondback rattlesnake—is one of the life-sized habitat displays in this hall. The king cobra, reticulated python, and boa constrictors from the Malayan and Amazonian jungle are among the large snakes on view. Feeding habitats, locomotion methods, and the influence of human economics on reptiles and amphibians are also illustrated.

O. ORKIN INSECT ZOO

The whirls, chirps, buzzes, and rattles heard at the entrance to this hall are the sounds of the most abundant, diverse, and successful animals on Earth —insects and their relatives. One of the most popu-

•BELOW: In the O. Orkin Insect Zoo, visitors can explore the important roles of insects in ecosystems from rainforests, deserts, swamps and caves to suburban backyards.

•BOTTOM: The bite of most tarantula species is no more dangerous to humans than a bee sting. Visitors can see tarantulas in the insect zoo.

•OPPOSITE TOP: Two insect zoo visitors intent on a specimen.

•OPPOSITE BOTTOM: The cone-headed katydid blends in well with its surroundings.

lar attractions in the insect zoo is the walk-through tropical rainforest, with live giant cockroaches that in nature would dwell in the forest litter and tree hollows. Also in the rainforest are cave arthropods and other invertebrates. Caves teem with life forms that are attracted to year-round constant temperature and moisture.

The interactive exhibits and participatory activities in the insect zoo invite exploration and involvement by visitors of all ages. Children can crawl through a large model of an African termite mound, look into a real beehive, or touch a giant grasshopper. Visitors can hold some of the more docile animals in the zoo. Docents are available to answer questions. The popular tarantula feedings take place three times a day

NATIONAL MUSEUM OF AMERICAN HISTORY

Constitution Avenue between 12th and 14th Streets, NW

Mall entrance: Madison Drive between 12th and 14th Streets, NW

Open daily except December 25, 10 a.m. to 5:30 p.m.

(Extended spring and summer hours determined annually)

Metro station: Federal Triangle or Smithsonian

Smithsonian information: (202) 357-2700

Information recording in Spanish: (202) 633-9126

TTY: (202) 357-1729 (for visitors with communication impairments)

In 1858, the "objects of art and of foreign and curious research" in the National Cabinet of Curiosities were transferred from the U.S. Patent Office to the Smithsonian Institution. This was the genesis of the collections in the National Museum of American History. After the Centennial Exposition of 1876 closed, the Smithsonian received a windfall of objects that had been displayed in Philadelphia for the nation's 100th anniversary

NATIONAL MUSEUM OF AMERICAN HISTORY

?	Information	♦†♦	Restrooms
⌂	Checkroom	¶¶	Food Service
✚	First Aid	🏠	Museum Shop
▥	Stairs	♿	Accessible Entrance
⊞	Escalators	ℂ	Telephone
⊠	Elevators	⊠	Post Office
		★	Demonstrations
		$	Automated Teller Machine

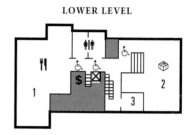

LOWER LEVEL

FIRST FLOOR

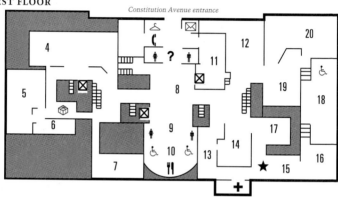

Constitution Avenue entrance

SECOND FLOOR

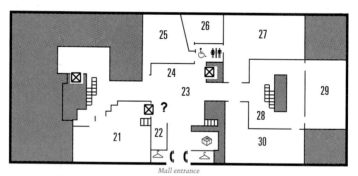

Mall entrance

THIRD FLOOR

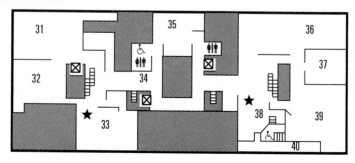

LOWER LEVEL
1   Cafeteria
2   Museum Shop & Bookstore
3   Security Office

FIRST FLOOR
(Constitution Avenue entrance)
4   Information Age
5   Science in American Life
6   Hands On Science Center
7   Library
8   A Material World
9   Palm Court
10 Ice Cream Parlor
11 Carmichael Auditorium
12 Agriculture
13 Timekeeping
14 Engines of Change
15 Power Machinery
16 Bridges and Tunnels
17 Electricity
18 Railroads
19 Road Transportation
20 American Maritime
      Enterprise

SECOND FLOOR
(Mall entrance)
21 Field to Factory
22 Smithson's Photo Center
23 Foucault Pendulum
24 Star-Spangled Banner
25 American Encounters
26 Hands on History Room
27 After the Revolution
28 Ceremonial Court
29 From Parlor to Politics
30 First Ladies

THIRD FLOOR
31 Ceramics
32 Musical Instruments
33 Printing and Graphic Arts
34 Textiles
35 Money and Medals
36 Armed Forces
37 Archives Center
38 Gunboat *Philadelphia*
39 A More Perfect Union
40 Firearms

INFORMATION DESKS

Near the Mall and Constitution Avenue entrances

PUBLIC PROGRAMS

For information on concerts, lectures, films, and other activities, ask at the information desks.

TOURS AND DEMONSTRATIONS

Tours include Highlights, Field to Factory, and First Ladies. Schedules vary seasonally. Demonstrations include interpretive carts illustrating the Cotton Gin, Early Recorded Sound, and Electricity; Power Machinery; Printing and Graphic Arts; and 1776 (the story of the Revolutionary War gunboat *Philadelphia*). In the Hands On History Room, visitors may handle reproductions of historical artifacts, and in the Hands On Science Center, visitors can participate in experiments. Ask at the information desks for current times and topics, or call (202) 357-2700 or TTY (202) 357-1729. For special school and adult tours, call (202) 357-1481 or TTY (202) 357-1563, Monday through Friday.

WHERE TO EAT

A cafeteria is located on the lower level. The Palm Court on the first floor serves ice cream and light refreshments.

MUSEUM SHOP

For sale in the museum shop on the lower level are a wide variety of objects and publications relating to American history and civilization, along with postcards, slides, film, T-shirts, and posters. A smaller museum shop and a photo center, where visitors can buy film and drop it off for developing, are at the Mall entrance.

AT A GLANCE

The **Star-Spangled Banner**, the **Foucault pendulum**, the **first ladies' gowns**, **George Washington's uniform and tent**, **Edison's light bulb**, **Ford's Model T** —the list could go on and on in this wide-ranging, entertaining, and educational museum. On the first floor, the emphasis is on the history and social impact of science and technology. On the second floor, social and political history are the focus. Coins, ceramics, musical instruments, textiles, armed forces history, and printing and graphic arts are featured on the third floor.

celebration. Many of these objects were put on exhibit in the United States National Museum Building (now the Arts and Industries Building) when it opened in 1881. Today the spacious halls of the National Museum of American History are filled with exhibits that explore America's technological, scientific, cultural, and political history.

FIRST FLOOR

COUNTRY STORE POST OFFICE

To the left of the Constitution Avenue entrance is a country store that was located in Headsville, West Virginia, from the 1860s to 1971, serving as a post office about half those years. Brought to the museum lock, stock, and barrel (staples and sundries of a bygone era still line the shelves), it again functions as an official post office. Stamps, including special issues, may be purchased here, and mail that is deposited receives a unique, hand-stamped "Smithsonian Station" postmark.

A MATERIAL WORLD

The materials that compose an object can reveal a great deal about the people who made and used it, about their environment, their skills, and their values. This exhibition introduces materials that make up objects of everyday life and helps visitors look at other objects in the museum in new ways. What are they made of? Why? Why does it matter?

The exhibition includes a Materials Panorama that shows how the overall look and feel of our world have changed from the 1700s to the present; a Mate-

•TOP: The Palm Court creates a turn-of-the-century environment for rest, light refreshments, and music of the period.

•MIDDLE: The country store post office.

•BOTTOM: These mortars and pestles are made from a wide variety of materials.

rial Messages section that compares objects with similar functions but made of different materials; and New Materials, New Choices sections that consider the opportunities and unpredictable consequences of the invention or widespread use of new materials such as aluminum and plastics. Among the most interesting objects in the exhibition is *Swamp Rat XXX*, a top-fuel dragster designed and built by Don Garlits and made up of scores of materials, including stainless steel, titanium, gold, and Lexan. Two interactive videos,

• ABOVE: Don Garlits's top-fuel dragster, *Swamp Rat XXX*, is a great attraction in the exhibition "A Material World."

• BELOW: "Old Red," the International Harvester spindle cotton picker (1943), symbolizes the end of the old labor-intensive cotton culture.

Knowing Materials and *Analyzing Materials*, are also featured.

FARM MACHINES

A wooden plow of colonial times can be compared with later steel plows, the traditional cradle scythe and winnowing fan with a 20-mule-team Holt combine of 1886. The International Harvester cotton harvester ("Old Red") of 1943 symbolizes the transformation of the labor-intensive cotton culture to one dominated by machines. The internal-combustion tractors illustrate major developments, from the 1918 Waterloo Boy to the 1924 John Deere and a more recent International Harvester.

AMERICAN MARITIME ENTERPRISE

The history of waterborne commerce, both on the high seas and on America's lakes, rivers, and canals, is the focus of this exhibition. More than 100 ship models, from the *Mayflower* to huge modern cargo ships, are on display. Machinery salvaged from the U.S. Coast Guard tender *Oak* has been reassembled, enabling visitors to see a fully operational engine room dating from the 1920s. There are separate displays relating to disasters at sea, shipbuilding during the world wars, whaling, luxury liners, and the seaman's life.

ROAD VEHICLES

Rarities from the museum's collection of more than 40 antique automobiles displayed here include the Duryea (1893) and the Haynes (1894); a 1903 Oldsmobile; a 1913 Model T

Ford; the 1903 Winton touring car; and a 1917 White motorbus. Also on exhibit are vehicles from earlier times, including a 1770 horse-drawn chaise and 19th-century carriages.

Cycles are here, too, the earliest a Draisine of 1818. In addition, there are velocipedes, high-wheelers, and safety bicycles. Among the motorcycles on view are the experimental 1869 Roper steam velocipede and a selection of vehicles manufactured during the first half of the 20th century.

• This exhibit in the American Maritime Enterprise hall re-creates a typical seamen's tattoo parlor.

RAILROADS

The big *1401*—a Pacific-type steam locomotive built for the Southern Railway in 1926—dominates this hall. The Pacific-type was once the most popular general class of passenger locomotive in the country. In contrast to the 280-ton *1401* is the *Pioneer*, a 12 1/2-ton engine of 1851, which served for nearly 40 years on the Cumberland Valley Railroad in Pennsylvania.

The eight-wheel passenger coach of 1836 is the oldest of its type in existence. Scale models are used to trace the development of locomotives and cars, while there are full-scale examples of braking apparatus, couplers, and signaling devices.

At one end of the hall is a Seattle cable car of 1888. Nearby is an 1898 electric streetcar from Washington, D.C., a diorama of New York's Third Avenue Elevated as it appeared in 1880, and models of other railborne vehicles used in urban transit.

BRIDGES AND TUNNELS

Displays show the changing techniques of bridge and tunnel construction from the Roman era to the present. There are models of famous bridges of various types—arch, truss, cantilever, and suspension. Models also illustrate the variations in tunneling technology. Three major timbering systems common in mid-19th-century tunnels are reconstructed at large scale.

POWER MACHINERY

The full-size engines and models displayed here illustrate the harnessing of atmospheric force, the early age of steam power, and the development of high-pressure and high-speed engines. Exhibits show

• TOP: The 280-ton Pacific-type steam locomotive *1401* was used on the Southern Railway between 1926 and 1951.

• BOTTOM: This electric streetcar was used on the Seventh Street line in Washington, D.C., from 1898 until it was retired in 1912.

the evolution of steam boilers and the steam turbine and progress in the techniques of harnessing waterpower. There are also a number of historic internal-combustion engines.

ELECTRICITY

The first part of this exhibition highlights electrostatics and the work of Benjamin Franklin. In a lighthearted tableau showing an 18th-century parlor trick, a woman receives an "electric kiss" from a man via a large electrostatic machine. Then the gallery traces the development of electrical power in the late 19th century, with special emphasis on the work of Thomas Edison.

TIMEKEEPING, PHONOGRAPHS, TYPEWRITERS, AND LOCKS

A variety of historic timekeepers—from sundials to atomic clocks—are displayed here, along with exhibits tracing the development of American clockmaking. Several early examples of sound-recording and reproducing machines are here, too, including one of Thomas Edison's first phonographs (1877), Emile Berliner's 1888 gramophone, and the Victor Talking Machine. Some of America's earliest typewriters are exhibited in chronological sequence, starting with a 19th-century reproduction of Burt's patent model of 1829. Many of the locks, keys, bolts, and other hardware shown are remarkable for the artistry that has been lavished on them.

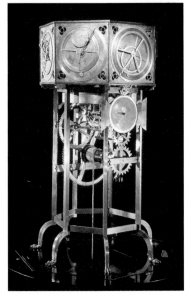

ENGINES OF CHANGE: THE AMERICAN INDUSTRIAL REVOLUTION, 1790-1860

With more than 250 original artifacts, this major exhibition brings to life the American Industrial Revolution. It tells the stories of craftspeople, factory workers, inventors, and entrepreneurs who made contributions crucial to our modern way of life.

The exhibition begins with a re-creation of the Crystal Palace, the site of the 1851 World's Fair in London, where the superiority of American technology first won international recognition. "Engines of Change" offers case studies of the evolving industrial society and the work culture that made this superiority possible. It also presents some of the innovations that spawned the Industrial Revolution—new machinery, interchangeable parts, and the factory system.

The Slater spinning frame, the world's oldest operable locomotive—the *John Bull*, and the Colt revolver are among the objects that illustrate the ingenuity of the age and the effects of industrialization on American life.

• TOP: The "electric kiss" tableau in the Electricity hall depicts an 18th-century parlor game with an electrostatic machine.

• BOTTOM: A reconstruction of the astronomical clock created by Giovanni de'Dondi of Padua about 1350.

• OPPOSITE: "Science in American Life" shows scientists launching a stratospheric balloon in Antarctica to obtain ozone readings.

SCIENCE IN AMERICAN LIFE

In modern America, science and society are inseparable. Over the last 125 years, scientific research and science-based technology have been the most powerful agents of change in American life, and science has grown into a complex enterprise interwoven with all aspects of our culture.

"Science in American Life" examines this interaction. Through artifacts, historical photographs, computer interactive areas, and multimedia technology, the exhibition focuses on many of the scientific issues, achievements, misunderstandings, and controversies that have shaped contemporary life.

The exhibition explores intersections of science and society, including the founding of a pioneering chemical laboratory in an American university; the use of experimental psychology and intelligence testing; science as a promoter and entertainer at the 1939 World's Fair; industrial science and the invention of nylon; the mobilization of science for World War II and atomic bomb research in the Manhattan Project; the growth of environmental awareness; and the new frontiers of biotechnology. An interactive area at the end of "Science in American Life" examines the ways in which shifting public needs, interests, and values will shape science and society.

HANDS ON SCIENCE CENTER

To help visitors understand how science works and discover how science and society interact, the Hands On Science Center invites them to learn science by doing. They can solve a crime using DNA fingerprinting methods, test for food additives and water purity, learn what a "gas" carbon dioxide is, use a Geiger counter to test for radioactivity in everyday objects, experiment with different methods to clean up an oil spill, discover the many ways plastics can be reused, and find out the ultraviolet rating for their sunglasses.

Working alone or with the center's staff, visitors age five and older learn the principles underlying these technologies as they experience the fun and excitement of experimental science.

• TOP: The Hands On Science Center invites visitors to try scientific experiments.

• MIDDLE: Learning new methods of information processing in 19th-century business is part of the "Information Age" exhibition.

• BOTTOM: The entrance to "Information Age."

INFORMATION AGE: PEOPLE, INFORMATION, AND TECHNOLOGY

Beginning with Samuel Morse's invention of the telegraph in the 1830s, this exhibition explores how information technology has changed our lives—as individuals and as a society—over the past 150 years. Objects such as Morse's telegraph, a piece of the first transatlantic telegraph cable, Alexander Graham Bell's original telephone, the early ENIAC computer, and modern microcomputers are on display, along with scores of video stations and computer-driven work stations. The exhibition also explores the influence of radio, television, wartime advances in information technology, the rise of the computer industry, and the spread of computer use into many sectors of modern life.

Throughout the exhibition and in a special gallery at the end, visitors can take advantage of dozens of interactive demonstrations and activities, including having their fingerprints taken, enciphering their names with the German ENIGMA encoder, seeing their voices graphically displayed on computer voice-recognition equipment, and producing an evening news program.

SECOND FLOOR

STAR-SPANGLED BANNER

Visitors entering the museum from the Mall encounter one of the nation's best-known patriotic symbols, the Star-Spangled Banner. This historic flag flew over Fort McHenry following the successful defense against British naval forces in September 1814. A lawyer named Francis Scott Key was aboard a ship in the Chesapeake Bay. When he saw that the "flag was still there" by the "dawn's early light," Key was inspired to write a poem that became the words to the national anthem. The flag is displayed with a curtain-like protective cover, which is raised and lowered hourly to musical and narrative accompaniment.

FOUCAULT PENDULUM

A crowd is always gathered in the center of the building to watch the

•ABOVE: The Foucault pendulum provides a visual demonstration of Earth's axial rotation.

•BELOW LEFT: The historic Star-Spangled Banner.

•BELOW RIGHT: Beautifully decorated Christmas trees are a holiday attraction at American History.

Foucault pendulum, patterned on an experimental device invented by a French physicist in the mid-19th century. Suspended from the ceiling of the fourth floor, a 90-kilogram (240-pound) hollow brass bob swings back and forth, knocking down, one by one, red markers arranged in a circle. Although the pendulum's vertical plane seems to change, in fact it remains fixed. What is actually changing its orientation is the floor, which "rotates" under the pendulum because of the Earth's rotation.

AFTER THE REVOLUTION: EVERYDAY LIFE
IN AMERICA 1780–1800

"After the Revolution" illuminates the lives of well-documented families and communities in the 1780s and 1790s. It begins with a multimedia program outlining the period and the three major groups that adapted to new ways of life—Native Americans, Europeans, and Africans, both slave and free.

Moving from rural to urban settings, the exhibition concentrates on the Delaware farm family of Thomas and Elizabeth Springer and their two daughters; African Americans in the Chesapeake area; the Virginia planter family of Henry and Ann Saunders and their daughter Betsy; the Seneca nation of the Iroquois Confederacy; the Massachusetts merchant family of Samuel and Lucy Colton; and the major urban center of Philadelphia.

The exhibition features the Springer log house and parlors appropriate for both the Saunders and Colton families, along with their furnishings. Tools, housewares, textiles, and ceremonial and religious objects document the blending of European and African traditions for African Americans; the struggle of the Seneca and other Iroquois peoples to maintain tradition in the face of radical change; and the great variety of trades, professions, and ways of life in Philadelphia, the country's major urban center in the last decades of the 18th century.

CEREMONIAL COURT

A White House welcome awaits visitors to the Ceremonial Court as they enter the re-created Cross Hall of the Executive Mansion. Dating from the 1902 renovation during Theodore Roosevelt's presidency, the original furnishings seen here include crystal chandeliers, enormous mirrors, mantels, pilasters, and plasterwork. Adjoining galleries showcase outstanding items from the national collections and pres-

●LEFT: The "Ceremonial Court" re-creates the Cross Hall of the White House at the turn of the century.

●BELOW LEFT: Dresses of the first ladies, from left to right: Eleanor Roosevelt, Mamie Eisenhower, and Jacqueline Kennedy.

●OPPOSITE TOP: This room from a two-story log house in Delaware that was the home of the Springer family in about 1790 is one of three family settings displayed in "After the Revolution."

●OPPOSITE MIDDLE: A parlor appropriate for the Coltons, a wealthy merchant family of Massachusetts, is also on view in "After the Revolution."

●OPPOSITE BOTTOM: Shown here are some Philadelphia artisans' silversmithing tools and examples of finished products.

idential memorabilia such as a pocket watch and telescope, Thomas Jefferson's lap desk, and Woodrow Wilson's golf clubs. Dolls, chess sets, and other toys of White House children are on view, as well as White House china, from George Washington's Chinese export porcelain to more contemporary patterns. Fine examples of American art glass, jewelry, red earthenware, silver, stoneware, and painted tinware are displayed. A floor-to-ceiling painting depicts Roosevelt children Archie and Kermit, playing on the grand staircase with their pet parrot Eli and their dog Jack.

FIRST LADIES: POLITICAL ROLE AND PUBLIC IMAGE

Through historic photographs, period graphics, gowns, and other personal artifacts, this exhibition traces the individual social and political accomplishments and interests of the first lady while underscoring her traditional responsibilities. The museum's renowned first ladies' gown collection is the centerpiece of this area.

FROM PARLOR TO POLITICS: WOMEN AND REFORM IN AMERICA, 1890–1925

The expansion of women's roles in shaping public policy is the focus of this exhibition. Organized around three domestic spaces—a parlor, a tenement, and Jane Addams's Hull House settlement in Chicago—it examines how women used the images and language of their homemaking and childrearing roles as a rationale for participating in political reform movements. The artifacts displayed include a hand-sewn temperance quilt, Susan B. Anthony's desk, and a ceramic model of the original Hull House building.

FIELD TO FACTORY: AFRO-AMERICAN MIGRATION 1915–1940

Between 1915 and 1940, more than one million African Americans left the South and headed north in search of a better life. This great migration was carried out by ordinary people making individual choices. "Field to Factory" looks at the hardships of southern life and its strengths; at the personal decisions to leave; and at city life in the North, where jobs were often menial and housing overcrowded, but where new communities and new racial pride emerged.

The exhibition features a Maryland sharecropper's house of about 1920; a replica of the separate entrances for whites and blacks at the Ashland, Virginia, train station; a video on the urban North; objects from a beauty salon run by Marjorie Stewart Joyner, one of the new black business owners; and a re-creation of a city rowhouse.

AMERICAN ENCOUNTERS

The arrival of Columbus in the Americas in 1492 began a series of global encounters between peoples of Africa, Asia, Europe, and the Americas that have in large part shaped the modern world. This exhibition explores one of those encounters that continues today. It began in 1539 in what is now New Mexico when Zuni Indians dis-

covered representatives of the Spanish government
seeking gold, silver, and souls in their land.

"American Encounters" examines some of the
ways American Indians and Hispanics have strug-
gled, fought, compromised, and learned to coexist,
first with one another and then with Anglo Americans, who came to the region in the early 1800s.
Visitors explore the Santa Clara Pueblo and the
practices of the Indians settled there since about
1350; attempts to Christianize the Indians; the
community of Chimayó, New Mexico, most of
whose people are descended from Spaniards who
settled in the valleys of northern New Mexico after
1695; the buying and selling of culture via the
tourist trade; and the concerns and struggles of Indians and Hispanics to maintain their distinct iden-
tities while living together in the American South-
west.

HANDS ON HISTORY ROOM

More than 30 activities built around reproductions
of historical artifacts offer a chance to touch, examine, and use objects similar to those elsewhere in
the museum. This is the place for everyone—adults
and children age five and older—to learn by doing
and get their hands on history. Activities include
pedaling a high-wheeler, sending a message by telegraph, turning the handle of a cotton gin, plucking
and striking keyboard instruments from the 18th
and 19th centuries, and studying the designs and
symbols on Zuni and Santa Clara pots, then deco-
rating a paper one. Young children especially will
enjoy Betsy's Moving Trunk, which lets them un-
pack the trunk of a little girl from a Virginia plantation and learn about life in the 1780s.

THIRD FLOOR

ARMED FORCES HISTORY

Uniforms, weapons, flags, and ship models illustrate the origin and growth of the armed forces and
the life of the citizen soldier. Highlights include
George Washington's field headquarters tent and a
Revolutionary War vessel—the Continental gunboat *Philadelphia*—dating from 1776, the oldest existing U.S. fighting vessel. Naval warship construction is examined through displays of ship models,
including the 1797 frigate *Constitution*, Civil War
ironclads, and the turn-of-the-century Great White
Fleet.

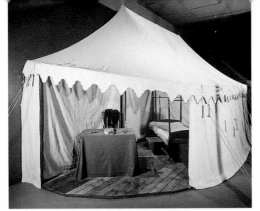

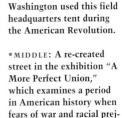

●TOP: General George Washington used this field headquarters tent during the American Revolution.

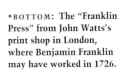

●MIDDLE: A re-created street in the exhibition "A More Perfect Union," which examines a period in American history when fears of war and racial prejudice led to the detention of some 120,000 Japanese Americans in camps across the West.

●BOTTOM: The "Franklin Press" from John Watts's print shop in London, where Benjamin Franklin may have worked in 1726.

• Fine musical instruments are displayed and exhibited in the Musical Instruments hall and gallery.

A MORE PERFECT UNION: JAPANESE AMERICANS AND THE U.S. CONSTITUTION

In the early weeks of World War II, the U.S. government forced some 120,000 residents of Japanese ancestry to leave their homes and go to detention camps for the duration of the war. Two-thirds were American citizens, and their rights and privileges under the Constitution were swept away. All were considered security risks.

This exhibition looks at prewar prejudice against Japanese Americans; the evacuation and relocation of men, women, and children; life in the camps; Japanese American troops defending the nation in combat; and Japanese Americans' efforts since the war to prevent another wholesale loss of liberties for themselves and for others.

Featured here are a copy of Executive Order 9066, signed by Franklin D. Roosevelt, that set the detention process in motion; a barracks room modeled after the Topaz Relocation Center in Arkansas; and *Conversations*, an interactive video that lets visitors select questions to be answered by people who experienced the detention camps.

PRINTING AND GRAPHIC ARTS

This hall deals with the history of prints and printing techniques. Settings feature a printing office of Benjamin Franklin's time, with two wooden presses; a 19th-century foundry in which type was still cast by hand, as it had been since Gutenberg's day; a job shop of 1865, equipped with hand and treadle presses; and an 1880s newspaper office with a steam-driven Hoe cylinder press. There are also exhibits on print-making, from the first etchings and woodcuts to modern photomechanical methods.

MUSICAL INSTRUMENTS

Displayed in a setting that includes an intimate hall used for concerts and recordings are exquisite examples of Western European and American instruments dating to the 17th century. Some have been carefully restored to playing condition. In addition to a permanent display of organs, harpsichords, and pianos, there are changing exhibits of stringed, wind, and percussion instruments used in various musical traditions.

CERAMICS

Selected for display from among the museum's excellent ceramics pieces are examples from the Hans Syz collection of 18th-century European porcelain, the Larsen collection of English earthenware decorated with American

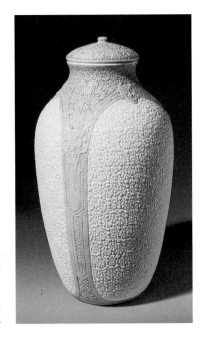

• An early gold coin depicting Alexander the Great.

views, American traditional pottery, tableware, art pottery, and the Leon collection of yellow-glazed English earthenware. Fine examples from Meissen, Sèvres, Wedgwood, and other important manufacturers can be seen, along with works from Bennington, Baltimore, and Cincinnati.

TEXTILES

Clothmaking in the American colonies was an arduous process involving the transformation of raw flax and wool into finished fabrics for clothing and household goods. A variety of 19th-century American implements for making textiles are on display here.

Rarities include a hand-operated knitting frame from the 1700s and a French Jacquard-equipped loom of the 1840s. Shawls, coverlets, hand embroideries of the 18th and 19th centuries, Jacquard-woven coverlets and pictures, and other fine examples of historic textiles from the museum collections are featured.

MONEY AND MEDALS

The story that unfolds pertains to the evolution of monetary exchange. A special feature is the gold room. In addition to coinage and currency from many nations, the hall includes a coin collectors' browsing area.

FREER
GALLERY
OF ART

Jefferson Drive at 12th Street, SW

Open daily except December 25, 10 a.m. to 5:30 p.m.

Metro station: Smithsonian

Smithsonian information: (202) 357-2700

Information recording in Spanish: (202) 633-9126

TTY: (202) 357-1729 (for callers with communication impairments)

The Freer Gallery of Art opened in 1923 as the first national museum of fine arts. Its collection of Asian art is generally acknowledged to be among the world's finest. The gallery's Asian collections, produced over six millenniums, represent the creative traditions of China, Japan, Korea, South and Southeast Asia, and the Near East. There are also examples of ancient Egyptian and early Christian art. The select collection of 19th- and early 20th-century American art includes the world's largest

FREER GALLERY OF ART

- ? Information
- Checkroom
- Stairs
- Elevators
- Restrooms
- Tour Meeting Point
- Museum Shop
- Accessible Entrance/Route
- Telephone

1–4	American Art
5–7	Japanese Art
8	Japanese Art
9	Korean Art
10–11	Chinese Art
12	The Peacock Room
13–16	Chinese Art
17	Buddhist Art
18	South Asian Art
19	Islamic Art
20	Courtyard

To travel between floors, it may be necessary to use two different elevators. Take elevator A to get to the accessible exit and exhibition galleries. Take elevator B to get to the Freer Gallery Shop and to the Arthur M. Sackler Gallery. The Meyer Auditorium can be reached from either elevator.

LEVEL 3

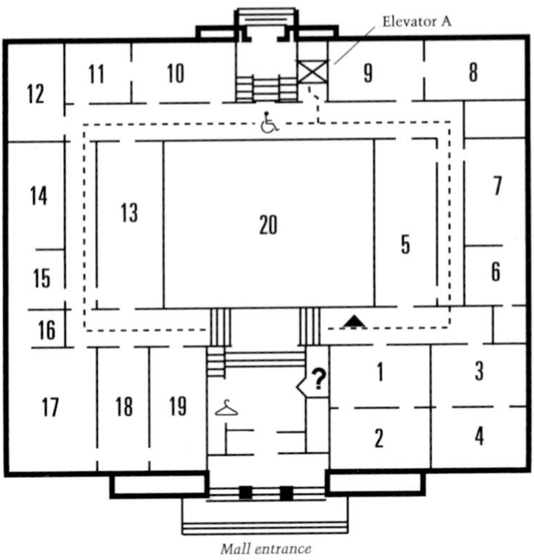
Independence avenue entrance
Elevator A
1
2
3
4
5
6
7
8
9
10
11
12
13
14
15
16
17
18
19
20
?
Mall entrance

LEVELS 1 AND 2

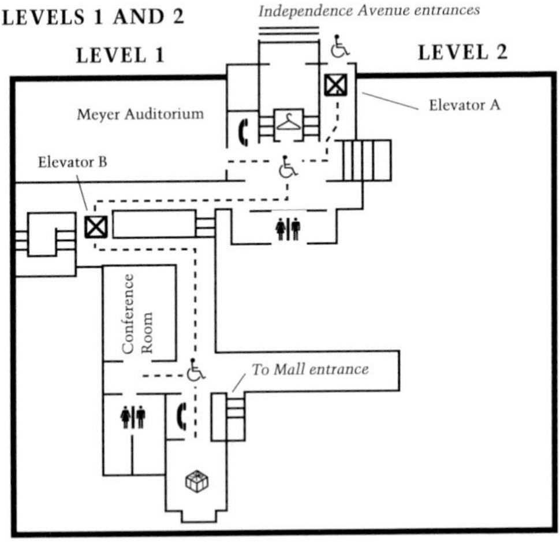
Independence Avenue entrances
LEVEL 1
LEVEL 2
Meyer Auditorium
Elevator A
Elevator B
Conference Room
To Mall entrance

LEVEL S

Connecting level to the Arthur M. Sackler Gallery

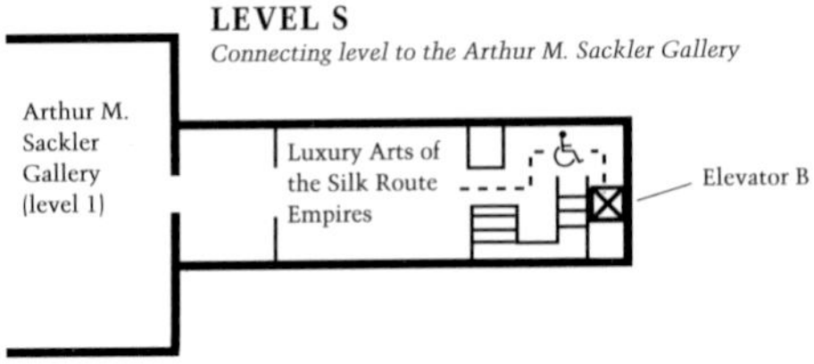
Arthur M. Sackler Gallery (level 1)
Luxury Arts of the Silk Route Empires
Elevator B

ENTRANCES

The main visitors' entrance is located on Jefferson Drive, SW. The street-level entrance on Independence Avenue has elevator service to the galleries. The nearby Arthur M. Sackler Gallery is accessible through an underground gallery space.

INFORMATION DESK

In the lobby near the Jefferson Drive entrance

TOURS

Free guided tours are given daily at specific times. Confirm walk-in tour times at the information desk, or call (202) 357-2700; TTY: (202) 357-1729. Request special group tours in writing at least four weeks in advance. Write to: Tours, Freer Gallery of Art, Smithsonian Institution, Washington, D.C. 20560.

GALLERY SHOP

Museum reproductions, books, posters, prints, jewelry, cards, and gifts are for sale in the shop on the Freer's second level.

LIBRARY

A library serving the Freer and Sackler Galleries is located on the second level of the Sackler. The library has nearly 60,000 volumes, about half of them in Chinese and Japanese, and subscribes to more than 400 periodicals. Researchers use a special study facility to examine the more than 100,000 photographic images in the archives. About 73,000 slides are available on loan for use in classrooms and lecture halls. Library hours are 10 a.m. to 5 p.m., Monday through Friday. Appointments are necessary to use the Archives and Slide Library; call (202) 357-4880.

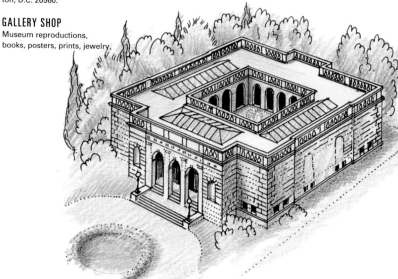

AT A GLANCE

The Freer Gallery of Art has one of the finest collections of **Asian art** in the world. These magnificent holdings, which span Neolithic times to the early 20th century, share exhibition space in the Italian Renaissance–style building with a major group of 19th- and early 20th-century American art. The Freer Gallery houses the world's most comprehensive collection of works by James McNeill Whistler, including **Harmony in Blue and Gold: The Peacock Room**, the artist's only existing interior design scheme, permanently installed in the Freer.

and most important group of works by James Mc-Neill Whistler (1834–1903). Since only a small part of the permanent collection can be shown at one time, changing selections of art are presented on a rotating schedule.

The gallery is named for Charles Lang Freer (1854–1919), a Detroit industrialist, and its unusual combination of creative traditions—Asian and American—reflect his preference. Charles Freer collected work by American artists, often his friends, whose styles and subject matter he believed complemented the refined qualities of the master-pieces of Asian art he began collecting after a trip to Asia in 1895. He wrote that he attempted to "gather together objects of art covering various periods of production, all of which are harmonious and allied in many ways."

• **Enamel and gold box, India, ca. 1650**

At his death in 1919, Freer left 7,500 Asian paintings, sculpture, and drawings; and works of calligraphy, metal, lacquer, and jade to form the Freer collection. Many other generous donors have since participated in the growth of the Asian collection, which now numbers 26,500 objects. Freer asked

• *Portrait of a Painter*, color and gold on paper, Turkey, late 15th century

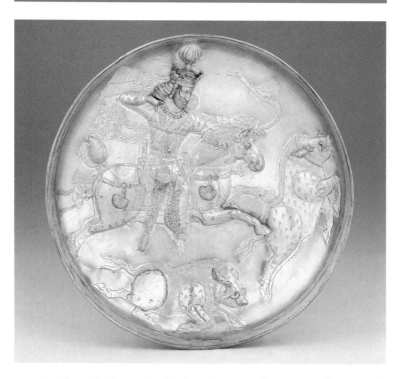

• ABOVE: **Silver and gilt plate, Iran, 4th century**

• BELOW: *Travelers in the Mountains of Shu*, **detail of a handscroll, China, mid-16th century**

that his American collection remain as he presented it, with some 1,500 works by artists whom he knew personally and whose work he admired. The American collection has long been an inspiration for original research by scholars from many nations.

With his collections, Freer gave the funds for a building to house them. He believed the Italian Renais-

DIRECTOR'S BEST

• *Queen Sembiyan Mahadevi as the Goddess Parvati;* bronze, India, ca. 950-1000 (Gallery 18)

• *The Ramayana (Story of Rama);* bound manuscript, opaque watercolor and gold on paper, India, ca. 1597-1605 (Gallery 18)

• Bowl; earthenware painted under glaze, inscription reads: "It is said that he who thinks one opinion is enough runs a grave risk. Blessing to the owner," Iran, 10th century (Gallery 19)

• Ritual wine server, *gong;* bronze, China, ca. 1100-1050 B.C. (Gallery15)

• Canteen; brass, hammered and turned or polished on lathe, chased and inlaid with silver and black organic material, probably Syria, mid-13th century (Gallery 11)

—Milo Beach, Director, Freer Gallery of Art

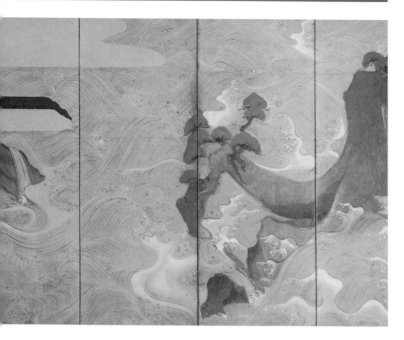

•OPPOSITE TOP LEFT: Carved box, buff, green, and red lacquer on wood, China, 1736–96

•ABOVE: *Waves at Matsushima*, one of a pair of six-fold screens by Tawaraya Sotatsu, Japan, 17th century

•OPPOSITE BOTTOM: Stoneware jar with cobalt pigment painted under colorless glaze, Vietnam, 15th century

•RIGHT: A detail of the northeast corner of *Harmony in Blue and Gold: The Peacock Room*, the only existing interior design scheme by James McNeill Whistler (American, 1834–1903) and an icon of the Freer Gallery of Art

sance style would provide an appropriate setting for the display of his art, and he worked closely on the plans for the building with the architect he chose, Charles A. Platt. Today the building is on the National Register of Historic Places. It is connected by an underground exhibition space to the nearby Arthur M. Sackler Gallery, also a Smithsonian museum of Asian art.

Exhibitions include American art, Japanese art, Korean ceramics, Chinese painting, Whistler's *Harmony in Blue and Gold: The Peacock Room*, ancient Chinese art, Buddhist art, South Asian art, Islamic art, Egyptian glass, and "Luxury Arts of the Silk Route Empires." A variety of free public lectures, concerts, films, and other programs complement these exhibitions.

ARTHUR M. SACKLER GALLERY

1050 Independence Avenue, SW
Open daily except December 25, 10 a.m. to 5:30 p.m.
Metro station: Smithsonian
Smithsonian information: (202) 357-2700
Information recording in Spanish: (202) 633-9126
TTY: (202) 357-1729 (for callers with communication impairments)

Founded in 1987 with a group of 1,000 master-
pieces of Asian art given by Arthur M. Sackler,
M.D. (1913–87), the Sackler Gallery is a leader in ed-
ucating the public about a continent that plays an
ever-larger role in the lives of Americans.

The gallery explores Asia's distinctive traditions
in a varied program of exhibitions from its own collection and others in the United States and abroad.
Archaeological riches lend variety to presentations

ARTHUR M. SACKLER GALLERY

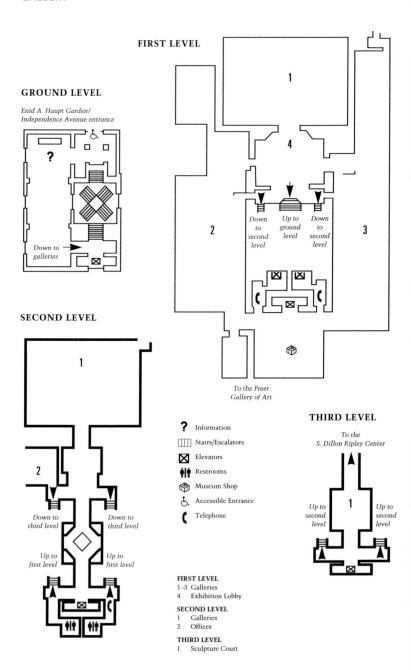

FIRST LEVEL

GROUND LEVEL

*Enid A. Haupt Garden/
Independence Avenue entrance*

?

Down to
galleries

SECOND LEVEL

Down to
third level

Down to
third level

Up to
first level

Up to
first level

Down
to
second
level

Up to
ground
level

Down
to
second
level

*To the Freer
Gallery of Art*

THIRD LEVEL

*To the
S. Dillon Ripley Center*

Up to
second
level

Up to
second
level

?   Information

▯▯▯   Stairs/Escalators

⊠   Elevators

♦♦   Restrooms

🏠   Museum Shop

♿   Accessible Entrance

℄   Telephone

FIRST LEVEL
1–3   Galleries
4   Exhibition Lobby

SECOND LEVEL
1   Galleries
2   Offices

THIRD LEVEL
1   Sculpture Court

ENTRANCE

Enter from Independence Avenue through a ground-level pavilion and then proceed to exhibition areas on two lower levels. The nearby Freer Gallery of Art with its related exhibitions and programs is accessible by an underground gallery space.

INFORMATION DESK

In the entrance pavilion

TOURS

Free guided tours are given daily at specific times. Confirm walk-in tour times at the information desk, or call (202) 357-2700; TTY: (202) 357-1729. Request special group tours in writing at least four weeks in advance. Write to: Tours, Arthur M. Sackler Gallery, Smithsonian Institution, Washington, D.C. 20560.

GALLERY SHOP

The shop, located on the first level, features quality merchandise based on the gallery's collection and various Asian cultures. Porcelain, crafts, jewelry, textiles, books, prints, and cards are available.

LIBRARY

A library serving the Freer and Sackler Galleries is located on the second level of the Sackler. The library has nearly 60,000 volumes, about half of them in Chinese and Japanese, and subscribes to more than 400 periodicals. Researchers use a special study facility to examine the more than 100,000 photographic images in the archives. About 73,000 slides are available on loan for use in classrooms and lecture halls. Library hours are 10 a.m. to 5 p.m., Monday through Friday. Appointments are necessary to use the Archives and Slide Library; call (202) 357-4880.

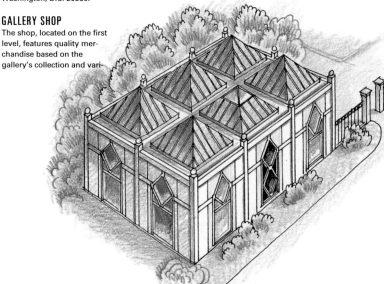

AT A GLANCE

The Arthur M. Sackler Gallery houses an important gift of Asian art from Arthur M. Sackler, M.D. (1913–87). Exhibitions from the permanent collection as well as international shows from Japan, China, Indonesia, Korea, India, Sri Lanka, and other nations trace the development of **Asian and Near Eastern art from ancient times to the present**.

*RIGHT: Bronze ritual wine server, China, 12th century B.C.

*BELOW: Japanese basket-maker Hiroshima Kazuo (b. 1915) was the subject of an exhibition at the Arthur M. Sackler Gallery.

*OPPOSITE: *Portrait of Yinziang, Prince Yi,* hanging scroll, China, Qing dynasty, 1644–1911

from different centuries and geographic areas, including art, crafts, and design in many mediums.

Exhibitions of work by living artists incorporate the artists' ideas—captured in writing, on videotape, and in person—and have included such diverse examples as animal paintings by a young Chinese girl and baskets by an 80-year-old craftsman from rural Japan. Some exhibitions and docent-led tours offer visitors the opportunity to touch objects and feel their weight and texture. A selection of masterworks by contemporary Japanese porcelain artists, for example, included pottery shards for visitors to handle. Reading areas furnished with educational materials are often included in the exhibition design.

Programs of film, music, dance, and drama present a broader survey of Asian culture. Outdoor dance and music performances attract crowds to the art inside. Members of local Asian communities often advise on and participate in the gallery's public programs. Regular public lectures reinforce themes introduced in the exhibitions or complement those topics with presentations of related research.

• *Creation*, porcelain bowl with polychrome enamel glazes, Tokuda Yasokichi (b. 1933), 1992

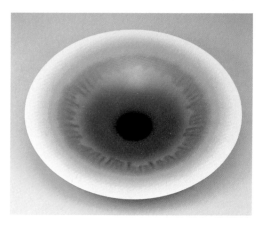

• *Men Exercise on the Sand Bank Facing Banaras*, photograph, Raghubir Singh (b. 1942), India, 1986

• *Shirin Presents a Jug of Milk to Farhad*, folio from a manuscript of the *Khamsa* by Nizami, Iran, ca. 1500

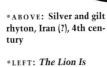

• ABOVE: Silver and gilt rhyton, Iran (?), 4th century

• LEFT: *The Lion Is Awake!*, ink and color on paper, Wang Yani (b. 1975), China, 1983

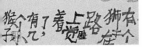

NATIONAL MUSEUM OF AFRICAN ART

950 Independence Avenue, SW
Open daily except December 25, 10 a.m. to 5:30 p.m.
Entrance: From Independence Avenue through the ground-level pavilion
Metro station: Smithsonian
Smithsonian information: (202) 357-2700
Information recording in Spanish: (202) 633-9126
TTY: (202) 357-4814 (for callers with communication impairments)

In African cultures, art is interwoven with daily life in ways quite different from most art in Western cultures. Religious beliefs and cultural ideals find artistic expression not only in masks and figures created primarily for ceremonial purposes, but in everyday practical objects. The main focus of the National Museum of African Art is collecting and exhibiting the traditional arts of Africa south of the Sahara. The museum also collects and exhibits the

NATIONAL MUSEUM OF AFRICAN ART

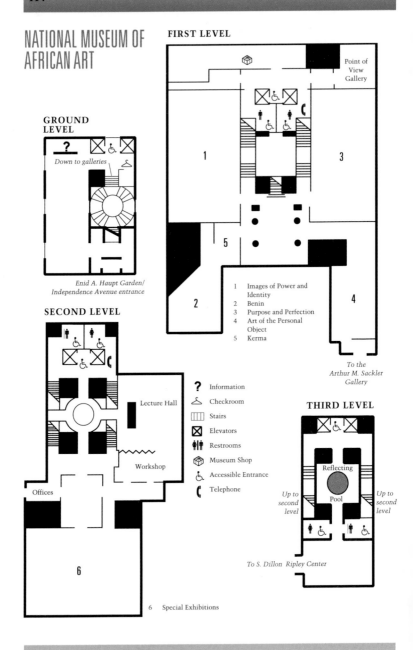

FIRST LEVEL

Point of View Gallery

1

3

5

2

4

1 Images of Power and Identity
2 Benin
3 Purpose and Perfection
4 Art of the Personal Object
5 Kerma

To the Arthur M. Sackler Gallery

GROUND LEVEL

?

Down to galleries

Enid A. Haupt Garden/ Independence Avenue entrance

SECOND LEVEL

Lecture Hall

Workshop

Offices

6

6 Special Exhibitions

? Information
⌐ Checkroom
▦ Stairs
⊠ Elevators
♀♂ Restrooms
🏠 Museum Shop
♿ Accessible Entrance
〖 Telephone

THIRD LEVEL

Reflecting

Pool

Up to second level

Up to second level

To S. Dillon Ripley Center

AT A GLANCE

The National Museum of African Art celebrates the **rich visual traditions and the diverse cultures of Africa**. Through its collections, exhibitions, research, and public programs, the museum stimulates appreciation of African art and civilizations.

INFORMATION DESK
In the entrance pavilion

TOURS
Free guided tours are offered
during the week and on the
weekends or by appointment
for adults and elementary and
secondary school groups. To
request a tour schedule or
make an appointment, call
(202) 357-4600, ext. 221; TTY:
(202) 357-4814.

MUSEUM SHOP
Books, exhibition catalogues,
postcards, posters, jewelry,
and other items are for sale.

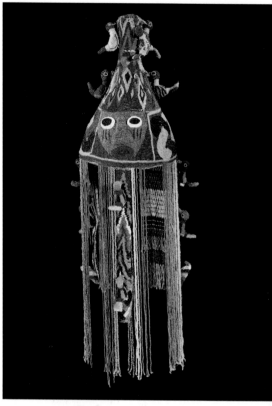

• A Yoruba artist from
Nigeria skillfully com-
bined brilliantly colored
glass beads to create this
extraordinary royal crown.
In Yoruba tradition,
strands of beads are the
emblems of the gods.
Wearing the beaded crown
with a veil is the quintes-
sential sign of kingship.

arts of other African areas, including northern Africa. Both ancient and contemporary arts are in the collection.

EXHIBITIONS

Exhibitions on the museum's first level are drawn from the expanding permanent collection. Works of art made of wood, metal, ceramics, cloth, and ivory are shown on a rotating schedule. The collection has particularly strong examples of royal Benin art;

•OPPOSITE TOP: This colorful flag (ca. 1935) made by Fante/Ghanaian artist Kweku Kakanu (born ca. 1910) with appliqué figures on both sides, was part of the regalia of a military company involved in the installation of paramount chiefs.

•OPPOSITE BOTTOM: *Pintades* (ca. 1950), a brilliantly colored painting by Zairian artist Pilipili Mulongoy (born ca. 1914) is an example of early modern African art.

•ABOVE: This beautifully carved mask of the Punu peoples, Gabon, symbolizes the afterlife and the spirits of the dead.

•BELOW: Cultural groups in eastern and southern Africa carved and used headrests in a variety of forms. The carver of this work (ca. 1890) of the Tsonga peoples, Mozambique and South Africa, displayed his considerable talents, artistic license, and sense of humor by rendering the elongated body of the elephant as a support for the headrest.

DIRECTOR'S BEST

At the National Museum of African Art, "The Art of the Personal Object" is an installation of more than 100 utilitarian objects, principally from eastern and southern Africa. This exhibition features stools and chairs, headrests, snuff containers, bowls and baskets. While many works by African artists are created for religious rituals or official ceremonies, the objects in this exhibition were created specifically for practical use in daily life. The works are outstanding examples of creative design. The artists who made these objects often worked within traditional local canons; however, their choices of materials, scale, proportion, detail, decoration and finish reveal their unique contributions.

—Sylvia H. Williams, Director, National Museum of African Art

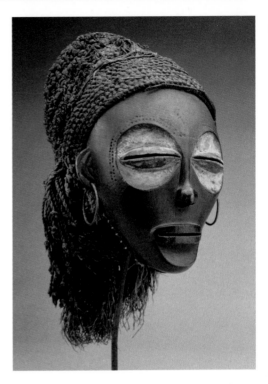

utilitarian objects such as stools, headrests, and personal objects; and central African ceramics. The museum also presents small exhibitions usually focused on works of art from the permanent collection. On the second level are a large gallery devoted to major temporary exhibitions, a lecture hall, an educational workshop, a library, and a photographic archives.

PUBLIC PROGRAMS

The African continent encompasses more than one-tenth of the world's population and approximately 900 distinct cultures. More than 25 million Americans trace their heritage to the cultures and traditions of Africa. With a variety of programs and resources for people of all ages, the museum is a bridge to the discovery of traditional African arts and cultures. It offers tours, lectures, hands-on workshops, musical programs, films, teacher training workshops, and audiovisual loan programs. Information about public programs and exhibitions is published in the museum's quarterly calendar. An annual educational programs brochure describing adult and school programs is also available. To be placed on the mailing list, write to: Calendar, National Museum of African Art, MRC 708, Smithsonian Institution, Washington, D.C. 20560.

• OPPOSITE: This mask of the Chokwe peoples of Angola depicts a young woman of great beauty. *Pwo* masks are used in public ceremonies, including postinitiation celebrations for young men.

• BELOW: This head of a ruler or a defeated chief, dating from the early period of court art in Benin, Nigeria (1350– 1550), is an outstanding example of the Benin bronzecaster's skill. Such commemorative heads traditionally were placed on ancestral altars.

RESEARCH FACILITIES

The National Museum of African Art is a leading research and reference center for the visual arts of Africa. The Warren M. Robbins Library, named for the museum's founder, contains more than 20,000 volumes on African art and material culture. The library is open from 9 a.m. to 5:15 p.m., Monday through Friday, by appointment; call (202) 357-4600, ext. 286. The Eliot Elisofon Photographic Archives, with 300,000 photographic prints and transparencies, extensive unedited film footage, and videos and documentary films on African art, specializes in the collection and preservation of visual materials on African art, culture, and the environment. The hours are from 10 a.m. to 4 p.m., Monday through Friday, by appointment; call (202) 357-4600, ext. 281.

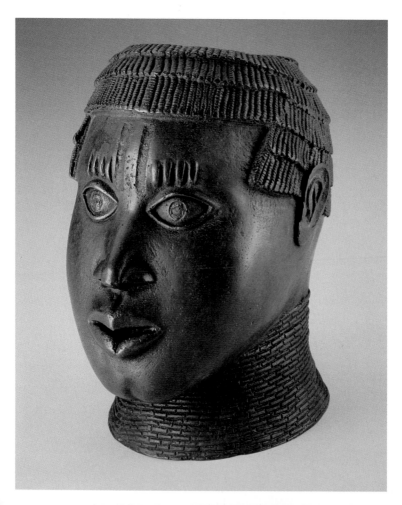

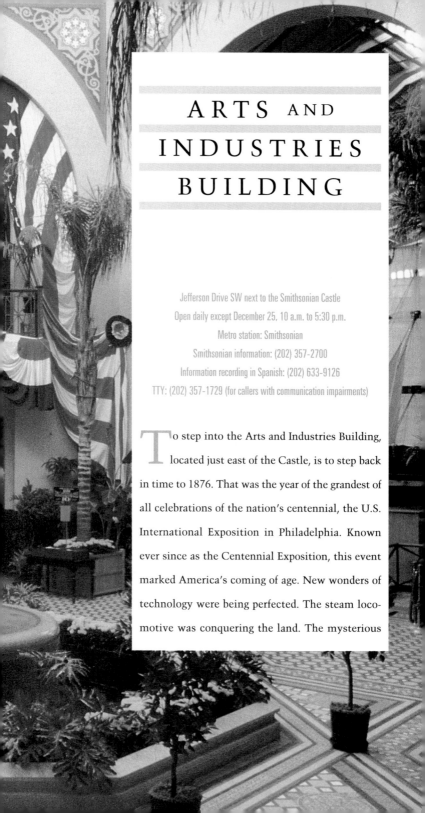

ARTS AND INDUSTRIES BUILDING

Jefferson Drive SW next to the Smithsonian Castle
Open daily except December 25, 10 a.m. to 5:30 p.m.
Metro station: Smithsonian
Smithsonian information: (202) 357-2700
Information recording in Spanish: (202) 633-9126
TTY: (202) 357-1729 (for callers with communication impairments)

To step into the Arts and Industries Building, located just east of the Castle, is to step back in time to 1876. That was the year of the grandest of all celebrations of the nation's centennial, the U.S. International Exposition in Philadelphia. Known ever since as the Centennial Exposition, this event marked America's coming of age. New wonders of technology were being perfected. The steam locomotive was conquering the land. The mysterious

ARTS AND INDUSTRIES BUILDING

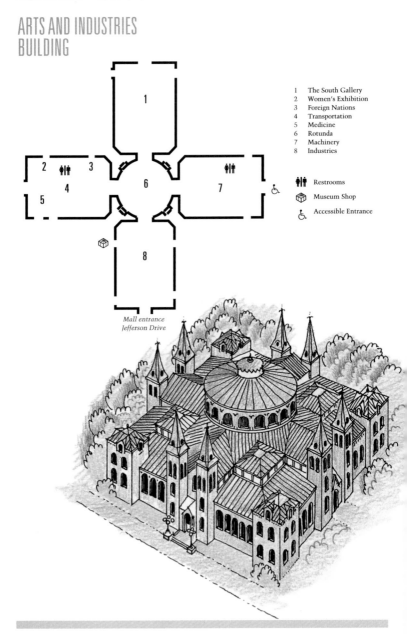

1 The South Gallery
2 Women's Exhibition
3 Foreign Nations
4 Transportation
5 Medicine
6 Rotunda
7 Machinery
8 Industries

👫 Restrooms

🏪 Museum Shop

♿ Accessible Entrance

*Mall entrance
Jefferson Drive*

AT A GLANCE

"1876: A Centennial Exhibition" displays thousands of objects in the style of the great Philadelphia Centennial Exposition, from which many of the exhibits were acquired. The temporary exhibitions in the South Gallery offer a glimpse of **African American history and life** as a unique feature of American culture. In the magnificent, light-filled rotunda of the building, a fountain is surrounded by flowers and plants that are changed seasonally.

INFORMATION DESK
At the entrance to the rotunda

TOURS
Docents give highlights tours of the exhibition on Saturdays only. For information, call (202) 357-2700; TTY: (202) 357-1729.

MUSEUM SHOP
Cards, books, jewelry, and items of Victoriana are featured. Merchandise from the Smithsonian mail-order catalogue is also sold in this shop.

DISCOVERY THEATER
Changing programs include presentations by mimes, puppeteers, dancers, actors, and singers. Performances are Tuesdays through Saturdays. For show times and reservations, call (202) 357-1500 (voice and TTY). Sponsored by The Smithsonian Associates.

forces of electricity were being harnessed. New mass production methods were bringing to everyone some of the conveniences that had been reserved for the few.

Three main halls of the Arts and Industries Building are filled with objects that actually were shown at the Centennial or are of a design and appearance appropriate to that period. There are steam-powered machines of every description—pumps, printing presses, machine tools, and dynamos. All sorts of manufactured goods are on display, from French lace to steel forgings, telescopes, a locomotive, silverware, perfume, and pistols.

THE BUILDING
This exuberant structure of red brick and Ohio sandstone, with its colorful maze of roof angles, towers, and clerestories, was designed by Washington architect Adolph Cluss. Completed in 1881, it is the second-oldest Smithsonian building on the National Mall. It was known originally as the United States National Museum, built to house objects given to the Institution after the Centennial Exposition closed.

Over the years, the Arts and Industries Building, as it was renamed, housed a variety of collections—including aircraft—that have since been moved to newer Smithsonian museums. In 1976 these fine halls, restored to the Victorian style, reopened for the nation's Bicentennial celebration, and Centennial-era exhibits were returned to display.

SOUTH GALLERY
The National African American Museum Project mounts changing exhibitions in the South Gallery. These exhibitions share aspects of African American history and life as a unique feature of American culture. For information about the current exhibition, call (202) 357-4500.

•PRECEDING PAGES: A view of the rotunda in Arts and Industries, decorated for the Bicentennial in 1976.

•LEFT: Clarissa Sligh, *Sandy Ground*, 1992–94

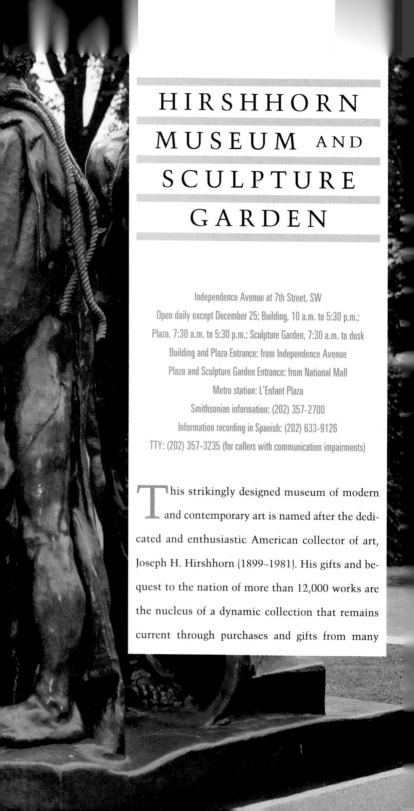

HIRSHHORN
MUSEUM AND
SCULPTURE
GARDEN

Independence Avenue at 7th Street, SW

Open daily except December 25; Building, 10 a.m. to 5:30 p.m.;

Plaza, 7:30 a.m. to 5:30 p.m.; Sculpture Garden, 7:30 a.m. to dusk

Building and Plaza Entrance: from Independence Avenue

Plaza and Sculpture Garden Entrance: from National Mall

Metro station: L'Enfant Plaza

Smithsonian information: (202) 357-2700

Information recording in Spanish: (202) 633-9126

TTY: (202) 357-3235 (for callers with communication impairments)

This strikingly designed museum of modern and contemporary art is named after the dedicated and enthusiastic American collector of art, Joseph H. Hirshhorn (1899–1981). His gifts and bequest to the nation of more than 12,000 works are the nucleus of a dynamic collection that remains current through purchases and gifts from many

HIRSHHORN MUSEUM AND SCULPTURE GARDEN

? Information

▥ Stairs

▦ Escalator

⊠ Elevator

♿ Accessible Entrance

🏪 Museum Shop

From lobby, down one level to:
- Ring Auditorium
- Self-Service Lockers
- Restrooms
- Telephone
- Drinking Fountain

LOWER LEVEL
Contemporary Art

SECOND FLOOR
Special Exhibitions

THIRD FLOOR
Modern Art

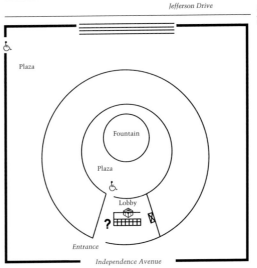

National Mall

(below street level)

Lehrman Pool

(street level)

Sculpture Garden

Jefferson Drive

7th Street

Plaza

Fountain

Plaza

Lobby

?

Entrance

Independence Avenue

AT A GLANCE

As the Smithsonian's showcase for modern and contemporary art, the Hirshhorn Museum and Sculpture Garden provides a comprehensive look at art from the first stirrings of modernism in the 19th century to the most recent developments in the art of our time. **Sculpture by modern masters** (much of it situated outdoors), **international modernist works of the postwar era,** and **contemporary art** are particular attractions. American and European variations on **Cubism, Social Realism, Surrealism, Geometric Abstraction,** and **Expressionism** trace modern art past the mid-20th century. Contemporary currents range from **Pop Art** of the 1960s to recent explorations by emerging artists working in a variety of media.

INFORMATION DESK

Located in the lobby and staffed until 4 p.m. daily. Exhibitions and events are posted here.

TOURS

Free, guided walk-in "orbit" tours are available Monday through Saturday at 10:30 a.m., noon, and 1:30 p.m., and Sunday at 12:30 p.m. Tours of large exhibitions on the second floor are available on Tuesday at 1 p.m. and Wednesday at 11 a.m. During May and October (weather permitting), visitors may tour the Sculpture Garden Monday through Saturday beginning at 12:15 p.m. Group tours, foreign-language tours, sculpture tours for the visually impaired, and sign-language tours can be arranged in advance through the Education Office. Call (202) 357-3235 (voice and TTY). All tours begin at the Information Desk; no tours are offered on national holidays.

CAFÉ

Full Circle, an outdoor, self-service, luncheon café on the museum's plaza, is open daily from late May through Labor Day weekend.

MUSEUM SHOP

Located on the plaza level, the shop offers exhibition catalogues, slides, postcards, reproductions, books on art, and other items related to the museum's programs.

PUBLIC PROGRAMS

A variety of free films, lectures, symposia, and talks by artists are presented regularly in the Marion and Gustave Ring Auditorium on the lower level. Other programs include staff gallery talks on individual artworks, family art-making workshops, seminars for high school students, contemporary music concerts (tickets required), and outreach programs for teachers and schools. For information, call (202) 357-2700; TTY (202) 357-3235.

●LEFT: David Smith (American, 1906–1965), *Cubi XII*, 1963

●BELOW: Auguste Rodin (French, 1840–1917), *Monument to the Burghers of Calais*, 1884–89

●RIGHT: Constantin Brancusi (Romanian, 1876–1957), *Torso of a Young Man*, 1924

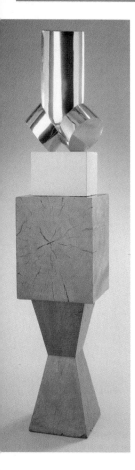

donors. When the museum opened in 1974, the Smithsonian offered, for the first time, a capsule history of modern art in a building and sunken garden that were bold, even daring, by contemporary architectural standards.

Today the museum is for many the most challenging and visually stimulating of the Institution's attractions on the National Mall. Museum goers may be dazzled or troubled by what is on view, but the experience is seldom boring. Art, especially new art, can evoke powerful responses.

Works from the permanent collection on public display are rotated, so what may be seen in any of the galleries at any given time will vary. In addition, important temporary exhibitions may fill certain galleries at different times.

SCULPTURE, INDOORS AND OUT

Sculpture was a special passion of the museum's founding donor, and the Hirshhorn's sculpture collection is one of the most distinguished in the world. Major works, primarily by European and American artists, range from mid-19th-century French bronzes to mixed-media installations by contemporary artists. Sculptures can be seen throughout the museum, its landscaped plaza, and the 1.3-acre Sculpture Garden along the Mall. Strolling through the garden, the visitor encounters bronze figures such as Auguste Rodin's *Monument to the Burghers of Calais*, Aristide Maillol's *Action in Chains*, and Gaston Lachaise's *Heroic Woman*, as well as Alexander Calder's colorful *Stabile-Mobile*, Henry Moore's intriguing organic compositions, and David Smith's geometric abstractions. Among the more recent, monumental sculptures displayed on the plaza are Claes Oldenburg's *Geometric Mouse* and Tony Cragg's witty *Subcommittee*.

Inside the museum, the circular ambulatories on the second and third floors offer an extensive overview of sculpture. The second floor traces developments in Europe from Jean-Baptiste Carpeaux and Edgar Degas through Henri Matisse and Ernst Barlach, while the third floor features modernist art from Pablo Picasso and Alberto Giacometti to David Smith and Robert Arneson. Sculptures in delicate materials, such as the poetic box assemblages by Joseph Cornell, are interspersed with paintings in the adjacent galleries.

MODERN ART

Currents in 20th-century art to the post–World War II era unfold in "The Collection Reviewed: Modern Art" on the third floor. Stressing an international mix of modern artists, the exhibition opens with

keenly observed scenes of American life, including
paintings by George Bellows, Thomas Hart Benton,
Edward Hopper, and artists of the Ashcan School,
together with Elie Nadelman's theater-inspired

• ABOVE LEFT: **Morris Louis (American, 1912–1962)**, *Where*, 1960

• LEFT: **Sigmar Polke (German, b. 1941)**, *Stairwell*, 1982

• ABOVE RIGHT: **Mary Cassatt (American, 1844–1926)**, *Young Girl Reading*, c. 1894

wood figures. Works by 19th-century precursors such as Mary Cassatt and Thomas Eakins are also frequently exhibited here. The stylistic innovations of first-generation modernists—such as Stanton Macdonald-Wright, Stuart Davis, and Marsden Hartley, each singularly inspired by Cubism—continue the procession, which also encompasses paintings by such American originals as Horace Pippin and Georgia O'Keeffe. The spread and consolidation of a modern approach during the 1920s and 1930s are revealed in the pristine styles of Fernand Léger and Constantin Brancusi, organic abstractions by sculptors Isamu Noguchi and Barbara Hepworth, and the literal and metaphoric Surrealism of René Magritte and Joan Miró. Vivid depictions of the figure by Europeans Francis Bacon, Balthus, Jean Dubuffet, and Lucian Freud make interesting comparisons with the visions of their postwar American contemporaries Clyfford Still and Willem de Kooning of the New York–based Abstract Expressionist group and Joan Brown and Richard Diebenkorn from the West Coast. Bringing the procession to about 1960, paintings by Morris Louis and Helen Frankenthaler show diverse approaches to color, structure, and form that feed the evocative powers of abstraction.

CONTEMPORARY ART

An emphasis on the "new"—newly conceived, newly created, newly acquired—characterizes "The Collection Reviewed: Contemporary Art," a selection of works from the 1960s to the present on the lower level. A journey through neo-Dada, Pop Art, Minimalism, and beyond leads from a significant early construction by Christo, in which the Bulgarian-born artist salvaged and "wrapped" the interior of a small-scale storefront, to Jan Vercruysse's wall sculpture of blue Venetian glass resembling a row of hanging Shaker chairs. The renowned American painter Jasper Johns is represented both by an early assemblage and a recent canvas that explores the ambivalence of perception. Works in diverse media by Julian Schnabel, Sigmar Polke, Anish Kapoor, Elizabeth Murray, Anselm Kiefer, Sam Gilliam, Rachel Whiteread, Glenn Ligon, Brice Marden, and others reveal the breadth and vitality of today's artists. Lower-level installations change periodically; contemporary art is also on view in selected galleries on the second and third floors.

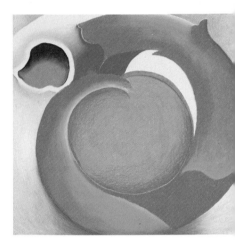

A NOTE ON THE ARCHITECTURE

Gordon Bunshaft (1909–1990), winner in l987 of the Pritzker Prize in architecture, designed the Hirshhorn complex. Redesigns of the Sculpture Garden in 1981 and the plaza in 1993 increased their accessibility and enhanced the placement of sculpture with additional greenery. The dynamic and unorthodox building—25 meters (82 feet) high and 70 meters (231 feet) in diameter—encircles an open courtyard and an asymmetrically placed bronze fountain. The exterior wall is a solid surface, broken only by a window 21 meters (70 feet) long in the third-floor Abram Lerner Room, from which visitors may enjoy a spectacular view of the National Mall. Floor-to-ceiling windows define the inner core, which overlooks the fountain. Four massive piers elevate the concrete structure above the walled plaza. The recessed garden across Jefferson Drive, with its rectangular reflecting pool, provides a peaceful area for viewing art. Outdoors at the Hirshhorn, benches, shaded areas, and fountainside tables at a summertime café provide attractive spots in which to linger and snack. Please enjoy—but do not touch the sculptures!

•LEFT: Georgia O'Keeffe
(American, 1887–1986),
Goat's Horn with Red,
1945

•RIGHT: Claes Oldenburg
(American, b. Sweden,
1929), *7-Up,* 1961

•BELOW: Francis Bacon
(British, b. Ireland, 1909-
1992), *Study for Portrait
of van Gogh III,* 1957

NATIONAL PORTRAIT GALLERY

8th and F Streets, NW

Entrance: On F Street

A 10-minute walk from the National Mall

Metro station: Gallery Place

Open daily except December 25, 10 a.m. to 5:30 p.m.

Smithsonian information: (202) 357-2700

Information recording in Spanish: (202) 633-9126

TTY: (202) 357-1729 (for callers with communication impairments)

A portrait, Thomas Carlyle believed, is "as a small lighted candle" by which biographies can "for the first time be read, and some human interpretation be made of them. . . . It has always struck me that Historical Portrait-Galleries . . . ought to exist . . . in every country, as among the most popular and cherished National Possessions."

The first official gesture toward creating a national portrait gallery in the United States was made

NATIONAL PORTRAIT GALLERY

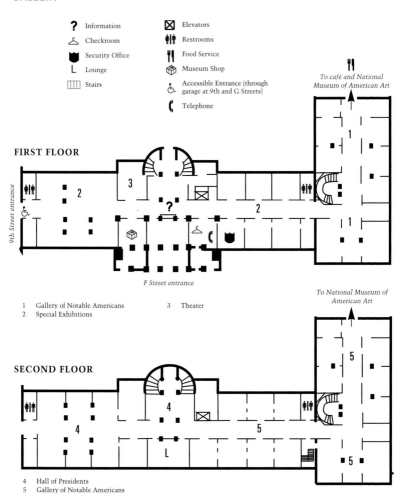

? Information
⊠ Elevators
Checkroom
Restrooms
Security Office
Food Service
L Lounge
Museum Shop
Stairs
Accessible Entrance (through garage at 9th and G Streets)
Telephone

FIRST FLOOR

9th Street entrance

F Street entrance

1 Gallery of Notable Americans
2 Special Exhibitions
3 Theater

To café and National Museum of American Art

SECOND FLOOR

4 Hall of Presidents
5 Gallery of Notable Americans

To National Museum of American Art

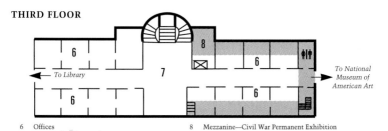

THIRD FLOOR

To Library

To National Museum of American Art

6 Offices
7 Great Hall and Rotunda
8 Mezzanine—Civil War Permanent Exhibition

INFORMATION DESK
At the main entrance (F Street)

TOURS
Free guided tours of the Hall of Presidents, the permanent collection, and special exhibitions are available on a walk-in or scheduled basis to individuals and groups. Ask at the information desk, or arrange in advance by calling (202) 357-2920, ext. 1.

MUSEUM SHOP
Exhibition catalogues, the *Illustrated Checklist* of the gallery's permanent collection, biography, history, and art books, posters, jewelry, tote bags, and scarves are for sale in the shop.

WHERE TO EAT
A small café on the first floor serves lunch daily.

PUBLIC PROGRAMS
A variety of programs, materials, and services are available. Cultures in Motion: Portraits in American Diversity brings the gallery's collection to life through lectures, symposiums, concerts, and other performance media. Biweekly film presentations focus on the lives and times of notable Americans. During Lunchtime Lectures, curators and other guests speak on topics related to current exhibitions. For more information, see the gallery's bimonthly *Calendar of Events*, or call the Education Department at (202) 357-2920.

RESEARCH SERVICES
The gallery offers research services by appointment, including the Office of the Historian, the Catalog of American Portraits, and the library. The National Portrait Gallery–National Museum of American Art library specializes in American art, American history, and biography. It is open to researchers Monday through Friday from 10 a.m. to 5 p.m. (except federal holidays).

AT A GLANCE

From Pocahontas to Bill Clinton, from George Washington to Eleanor Roosevelt, Albert Einstein, Robert Frost, and Martin Luther King Jr.—assembled at the National Portrait Gallery are **portraits of men and women who have** **contributed significantly to the history, development, and culture of the United States**. Special exhibitions, the Hall of Presidents, and the selections from the Civil War collection are not to be missed.

in 1857, when Congress commissioned G.P.A. Healy to paint a series of presidential portraits for the White House. In the decades following World War I, a national portrait gallery was seriously proposed as a part of the general art collection then developing within the Smithsonian Institution. The National Portrait Gallery of the United States was officially established by an Act of Congress in 1962 and opened to the public in 1968.

The gallery's holdings consist of paintings, sculptures, prints, drawings, and photographs depicting, as Congress directed, "men and women who have made significant contributions to the history, development, and culture of the people of the United States." The collections now number more than 16,000 objects.

With the exception of presidents of the United States, portraits are not admitted to the permanent collection or publicly displayed, except as part of a special exhibition, until 10 years after the subject's death. Under certain circumstances, however, the gallery may accept a portrait for later addition to the collection. The final decision on acquisitions rests with the National Portrait Gallery Commission. The gallery's preference is for likenesses taken directly from life, or for those that are at least contemporary with the subject.

Nearly two-thirds of the portraits now in the permanent collection have come as gifts, and the rest were purchased with funds appropriated by Congress for the overall operation of the gallery. Major loan exhibitions and smaller shows, assembled from collections both in this country and abroad, highlight themes from American history or the art of portraiture. Fully illustrated catalogues accompany all major exhibitions.

The National Portrait Gallery is also a resource center for biography and portraiture, offering research services by appointment through several offices.

•OPPOSITE TOP: **John Singleton Copley (1738–1815), self-portrait, oil on canvas, 1780–84 (gift of the Morris and Gwendolyn Cafritz Foundation with matching funds from the Smithsonian Institution)**

•OPPOSITE BOTTOM: **The Great Hall on the third floor of the National Portrait Gallery**

•RIGHT: **Abraham Lincoln (1809–65), watercolor on ivory by John Henry Brown (1819–91), 1860**

Extensive biographical files are kept in the Office of the Historian. The Catalog of American Portraits, a unique national reference center, documents more than 100,000 portraits of noted Americans that are located in public and private collections throughout the country. Researchers may use the files and request searches and reports from the online computer database. The library, shared with the National Museum of American Art, contains 100,000 volumes, receives more than 1,000 periodicals, and has an extensive collection of clippings and pamphlets on art subjects. The Peale Family Papers, devoted to research on the work and lives of this prominent Philadelphia family of artists and naturalists, provides information and materials relating to American cultural and social development from the mid-18th to the late 19th centuries.

•LEFT: Mary Cassatt (1844–1926), oil on canvas by Edgar Degas (1834–1917), ca. 1880–84 (gift of the Morris and Gwendolyn Cafritz Foundation and the Regents' Major Acquisition Fund, Smithsonian Institution)

•RIGHT: Casey Stengel (1890–1975), polychromed bronze by Rhoda Sherbell (b. 1938), 1981 cast after 1965 plaster

FIRST FLOOR

Immediately to the right inside the main entrance (F Street) is the information desk, the starting point for guided tours. Nearby is the Museum Shop. The museum's major temporary exhibitions are on view in the galleries to the left of the main entrance. Small rooms for special exhibitions are to the right, along with part of the gallery's permanent collection sections, including recent acquisitions, performing arts figures, and champions of American sport. A left turn at the far end of this corridor brings the visitor to the café.

SECOND FLOOR

The Hall of Presidents is at the west end, introduced by portraits of George Washington. The rest of the space is devoted to likenesses of notable Americans from the colonial period to the 20th century, including Benjamin Franklin by Joseph Siffred Duplessis, Mary Cassatt by Edgar Degas, and George Washington Carver by Betsy Graves Reyneau. In

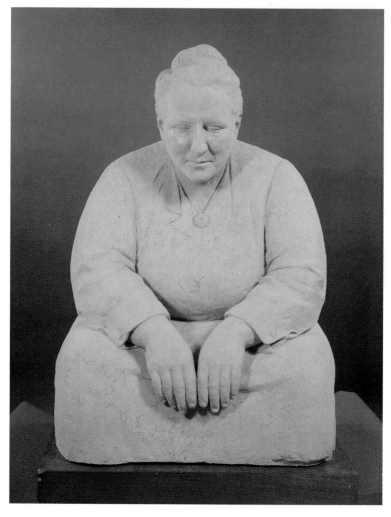

the second-floor lounge is a collection of Auguste
Edouart portrait silhouettes.

THIRD FLOOR

Selections from the gallery's Civil War collection
are displayed on the east mezzanine of the Great
Hall, including depictions of Frederick Douglass,
Harriet Beecher Stowe, Abraham Lincoln, Ulysses S.
Grant, Robert E. Lee, and Jefferson Davis.

•LEFT: Gertrude Stein (1874– 1946), terra-cotta by Jo Davidson (1883–1952), 1922–23 (gift of Dr. Maury Leibovitz)

•RIGHT: Henry David Thoreau (1817–62), daguerreotype by Benjamin D. Maxham (active 1854–59), 1856 (gift of an anonymous donor)

•BELOW: Frederick Douglass (1818–95), oil on canvas by an unidentified artist, ca. 1845

NATIONAL MUSEUM OF AMERICAN ART

8th and G Streets, NW

Entrance: On G Street

A 10-minute walk from the National Mall

Metro station: Gallery Place

Open daily except December 25, 10 a.m. to 5:30 p.m.

Smithsonian information: (202) 357-2700

Information recording: (202) 633-8998

Information recording in Spanish: (202) 633-9126

TTY: (202) 357-1729 (for callers with communication impairments)

The National Museum of American Art presents a panorama of American painting, sculpture, graphic art, photography, and folk art from the 18th century to the present. The collection has more than 37,500 works, ranging from 18th-century classical portraits through 19th-century sculpture, landscapes, and scenes of a developing land and its people, to the dynamic contemporary art of this

NATIONAL MUSEUM OF AMERICAN ART

FIRST FLOOR

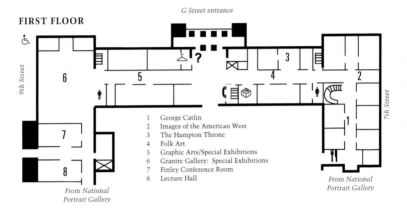

G Street entrance

1 George Catlin
2 Images of the American West
3 The Hampton Throne
4 Folk Art
5 Graphic Arts/Special Exhibitions
6 Granite Gallery: Special Exhibitions
7 Finley Conference Room
8 Lecture Hall

From National Portrait Gallery

From National Portrait Gallery

SECOND FLOOR

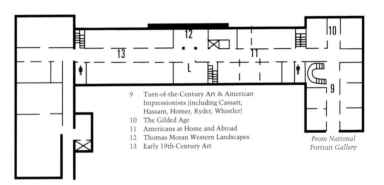

9 Turn-of-the-Century Art & American Impressionists (including Cassatt, Hassam, Homer, Ryder, Whistler)
10 The Gilded Age
11 Americans at Home and Abroad
12 Thomas Moran Western Landscapes
13 Early 19th-Century Art

From National Portrait Gallery

THIRD FLOOR

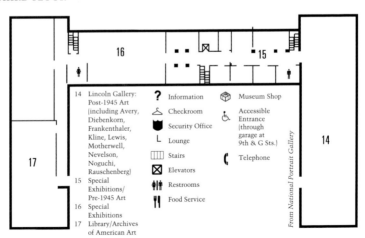

14 Lincoln Gallery: Post-1945 Art (including Avery, Diebenkorn, Frankenthaler, Kline, Lewis, Motherwell, Nevelson, Noguchi, Rauschenberg)
15 Special Exhibitions/ Pre-1945 Art
16 Special Exhibitions
17 Library/Archives of American Art

? Information
Checkroom
Security Office
L Lounge
Stairs
Elevators
Restrooms
Food Service

Museum Shop
Accessible Entrance (through garage at 9th & G Sts.)
Telephone

From National Portrait Gallery

INFORMATION DESK

At the main entrance (G Street)

TOURS

Free guided walk-in tours are at noon Monday through Friday and at 2 p.m. on weekends. Free gallery talks are given every Wednesday at 1 p.m. Group tours for students and adults may be arranged in advance. For reservations, call (202) 357-3111 or TTY (202) 357-4522. Sign language and oral interpreters are available on request for tours and public programs with one week's notice.

PUBLIC PROGRAMS

Free public programs include gallery talks, illustrated lectures, and family activities. For recorded information, call (202) 357-4511, (202) 357-2700, or TTY (202) 357-4522.

MUSEUM SHOP

The shop, near the main entrance, features museum publications and other art books, slides, reproductions, postcards, notecards, holiday cards, posters, calendars, jewelry, and unique gift items based on the collections.

WHERE TO EAT

A small café on the first floor serves hot meals, sandwiches, soups, salads, beverages, and desserts. The adjacent central courtyard is open for outdoor dining, weather permitting.

PRINTS AND DRAWINGS STUDY ROOM

This research facility is open by appointment. Call (202) 357-2593.

LIBRARY

The museum's library, shared with the National Portrait Gallery, specializes in American art, American history, and biography and contains more than 100,000 volumes. It is open to adults with research projects or inquiries. It is open to researchers Monday through Friday from 10 a.m. to 5 p.m. (except federal holidays). Call (202) 357-1886.

ELECTRONIC RESOURCES

The museum makes hundreds of images from the collection and extensive information on its collections, publications, and activities available to personal computer users on the Internet (gopher and ftp sites at *nmaa-ryder.si.edu* and World Wide Web site at *http://www.nmaa.si.edu)* and commercial online services.

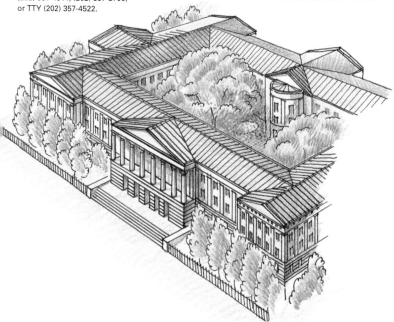

AT A GLANCE

The nation's oldest federal art collection presents **more than 250 years of American painting, sculpture, folk art, photography, and graphic art.** Changing selections from the permanent collection are on view. The museum presents about 15 temporary exhibitions each year in galleries on the first and third levels. The magnificent **Lincoln Gallery** on the third floor was the site of Abraham Lincoln's 1865 inaugural reception.

century. American crafts are featured at the Renwick Gallery of the National Museum of American Art (see page 154).

Changing selections from the permanent collection are on display on all three floors of the museum. Temporary exhibitions on various aspects of American art, often accompanied by publications and interactive computer programs, are drawn from the permanent collection and often circulated to museums and university galleries throughout the United States. Works of art not on display are available for study by visiting scholars.

As a major center for research in American art, the museum includes such resources as the Inventory of American Paintings Executed Before 1914, with data on nearly 260,000 works; the Peter A. Juley & Sons collection of 127,000 historic photographs; the Slide and Photographic Archives; the Smithsonian Art Index; the Pre-1877 Art Exhibition Catalogue Index; the Inventory of American Sculpture, with information on more than 50,000 indoor and outdoor works; and the Joseph Cornell Study Center.

The library, shared with the National Portrait Gallery, contains more than 100,000 volumes on art, history, and biography, with special emphasis on the United States. It also houses the Archives of American Art, with its vast holdings of documentary material on American art and artists.

•OPPOSITE TOP: **Luis Jiménez (b. 1940), *Vaquero*, 1980** (gift of Judith and Wilbur Ross, Jr., Anne and Ronald Abramson, Thelma and Melvin Lenkin)

•OPPOSITE BOTTOM: **Edward Hopper (1882-1967), *Cape Cod Morning*, 1950** (gift of the Sarah Roby Foundation)

•ABOVE: **Abbott Handerson Thayer (1849-1921), *Angel*, 1889** (gift of John Gellatly)

COLLECTIONS

Both famous and lesser-known American artists are represented. Among the earlier artists are Albert Bierstadt, Asher B. Durand, Frederic Edwin Church, Ralph Earl, Winslow Homer, Thomas Moran, Charles Willson Peale, Thomas Cole, and Benjamin West. The museum boasts the most comprehensive collections of African American art and federally sponsored WPA art in the country, a major collection of American folk art, and a growing collection of American photography dating from the inception of the medium to the present. The museum also holds some 445 paintings of Native Americans by George Catlin from the collection he showed in Paris in the 1840s.

Twentieth-century painting and sculpture are represented by artists such as Franz Kline, Willem de Kooning, Romaine Brooks, Edward Hopper, William H. Johnson, Georgia O'Keeffe, Morris Louis, Robert Rauschenberg, and Paul Manship.

A major mural by Thomas Hart Benton hangs in the lobby area. Recent acquisitions are also exhibited there. Among other works on the first floor are folk art objects (number 4 on map), including the well-known *Throne of the Third Heaven* assemblage by James Hampton (3 on map), and images of Native Americans and the American West by Frederic Remington, John Mix Stanley, and George

• ABOVE: **Albert Bierstadt**
(1830-1902), *Among the*
Sierra Nevada Mountains,
California, **1868 (bequest**
of Helen Huntington Hull)

• LEFT: **Albert Pinkham**
Ryder (1847-1917),
Moonlight, **1880-85 (gift of**
William T. Evans)

• RIGHT: **Charles Willson**
Peale (1741-1827), minia-
ture portrait of Matthias
and Thomas Bordley, 1767
(museum purchase and gift
of Mr. and Mrs. Murray
Lloyd Goldsborough, Jr.)

DIRECTOR'S BEST

• *The Flying Dutchman* and
Jonah, by Albert Pinkham
Ryder, 1887 and ca. 1885
Of all my personal favorites
in the museum, the paintings
of Albert Pinkham Ryder are
first. In these paintings of
churning seas, Ryder mar-
shals extraordinary rhythmic
forces. His broad, slashing
lines and energetic brush-
work hint that, well ahead
of his time, he was as interested in the process of
painting as rendering the
narrative image.

• *Interior With Portraits,* by
Thomas LeClear, ca. 1865
This posthumous portrait of
a brother and sister having
their photograph taken in a
studio cleverly alludes to the
debate on the merits of photography versus painting in

the early days of the camera.

• *Elizabeth Winthrop Chanler*
(Mrs. John Jay Chapman),
by John Singer Sargent,
1893
Sargent's 26-year-old subject sits between paintings
of a madonna and child and
an old woman. Did he inten-
tionally fix this then unmar-
ried woman halfway
between motherhood and
old age?

• *The Sick Child,* by J. Bond
Francisco, 1893
In the 19th century, infant
and child mortality was a
distressingly common part
of life. In this beautifully
composed picture, the artist
leaves us in doubt about
whether this feverish boy
will survive.

—Elizabeth Broun, Director,
National Museum of American Art

Catlin (1 on map). The Graphic Arts gallery (5) presents changing exhibitions of prints and drawings.

The second floor features a survey of early 19th-century paintings and sculpture and a large and choice group of oil paintings by Albert Pinkham Ryder and Winslow Homer. Among the works of American impressionists (9) are paintings by Mary Cassatt, Childe Hassam, John Twachtman, and William Merritt Chase. The lobby (12) features three massive Thomas Moran paintings of the Grand Canyon that represent the grand flowering of American landscape painting.

Also on the second floor are 19th-century paintings and sculpture by John Singer Sargent, Daniel Chester French, Augustus Saint-Gaudens, Frederic Edwin Church, and John Frederick Kensett. In the Turn-of-the-Century galleries are paintings by Thomas Wilmer Dewing, Julian Alden Weir, and James McNeill Whistler, and a stunning stained glass window by John La Farge.

The third floor is devoted to the 20th century, with changing installations of work of the 1930s and the Federal Art Project. Among the artists represented are Charles Sheeler, Paul Cadmus, and Paul Manship. Works by early modernists include Stuart Davis and John Sloan. In the historic Lincoln Gallery (14) are paintings and sculptures from the postwar era to the present, including works by Kenneth Noland, Morris Louis, Gene Davis, Louise Nevelson, Isamu Noguchi, Clyfford Still, and Nam June Paik.

•ABOVE: Thomas Hart Benton (1889-1975), *Achelous and Hercules*, 1947 (gift of Allied Stores Corporation and museum purchase through Major Acquisitions Fund, Smithsonian Institution)

•BELOW: William H. Johnson (1901-1970), *Man in a Vest*, 1939-40 (gift of the Harmon Foundation)

•RIGHT: Romaine Brooks (1874-1970), *Una, Lady Troubridge*, 1924 (gift of the artist)

HISTORY

The National Museum of American Art, the oldest national art collection in the United States, predates the founding of the Smithsonian Institution. It moved into its first permanent home, the historic Old Patent Office Building, in May 1968. The building is one of the nation's best examples of neoclassical architecture and a particularly appropriate location for the museum since the beginnings of the collection were exhibited here as early as 1841.

In 1829 a Washingtonian named John Varden began a collection he deemed fitting for the nation's capital. This collection—from which some works remain—was absorbed into the National Institute, which displayed its works of art beside those belonging to the government in the third-floor galleries of the then-new Patent Of-

fice. Paintings and sculpture shared exhibition space with the original Declaration of Independence, shrunken heads, Benjamin Franklin's printing press, stuffed birds, and George Washington's commission as commander of the Continental forces. In 1858 the collection belonging to the government was transferred to the Smithsonian Institution and, in 1862, the National Institute collection—including that of John Varden —followed.

The collection was named the National Gallery of Art in 1906, and it acquired paintings, sculpture, and memorabilia from Harriet Lane Johnston, the niece of President James Buchanan. The expanding collection was given a hall in the National Museum of Natural History when it opened in 1909. As that space became crowded, the art was either stored or lent to government offices throughout Washington.

Although the museum's history spans 150 years—including its designation as the National Gallery of Art until 1937 when that name was transferred to the Andrew Mellon collection—its works never had been shown properly until it moved into the Old Patent Office Building. From 1937 until 1980, the museum was known as the National Collection of Fine Arts. In October 1980, to reflect its decades-old policy of acquiring only American art, its name was changed to the National Museum of American Art.

Many major gifts and acquisitions of paintings, prints, photographs, folk art, decorative arts, and sculpture have been added to the collection over the years. Today the museum displays an exceptional selection of the wealth and variety of works created by American artists.

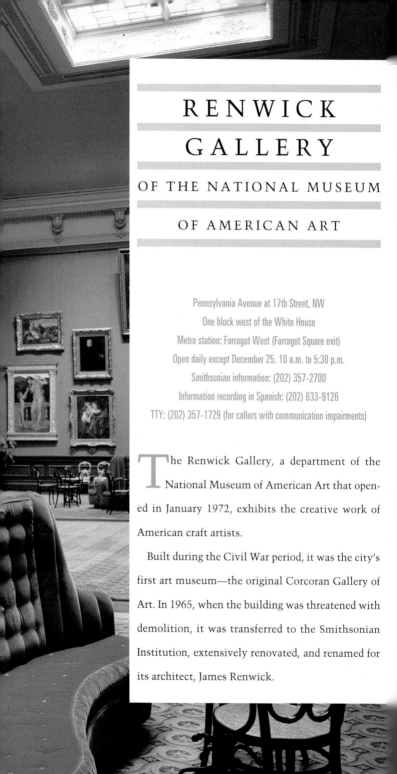

RENWICK GALLERY

OF THE NATIONAL MUSEUM

OF AMERICAN ART

Pennsylvania Avenue at 17th Street, NW
One block west of the White House
Metro station: Farragut West (Farragut Square exit)
Open daily except December 25, 10 a.m. to 5:30 p.m.
Smithsonian information: (202) 357-2700
Information recording in Spanish: (202) 633-9126
TTY: (202) 357-1729 (for callers with communication impairments)

The Renwick Gallery, a department of the National Museum of American Art that opened in January 1972, exhibits the creative work of American craft artists.

Built during the Civil War period, it was the city's first art museum—the original Corcoran Gallery of Art. In 1965, when the building was threatened with demolition, it was transferred to the Smithsonian Institution, extensively renovated, and renamed for its architect, James Renwick.

INFORMATION DESK
At the entrance

TOURS
Group tours for students and adults may be arranged in advance. For reservations, call (202) 357-2531 or TTY (202) 357-4522. Sign language and oral interpreters are available on request for tours and public programs with one week's notice.

PUBLIC PROGRAMS
Free public programs include craft demonstrations, gallery talks, films, and illustrated lectures. For recorded information, call (202) 357-2700 or TTY (202) 357-4522.

MUSEUM SHOP
The museum shop features Renwick publications and other craft and decorative art books, craft objects relating to exhibitions, postcards, note cards, holiday cards, posters, calendars, and jewelry.

ELECTRONIC RESOURCES
The museum makes hundreds of images from the collection and extensive information on its collections, publications, and activities available to personal computer users on the Internet (gopher and ftp sites at *nmaa-ryder.si.edu* and World Wide Web site at *http://www.nmaa.si.edu*) and commercial online services.

AT A GLANCE

Changing exhibitions of **American crafts and decorative arts**—historic and contemporary as well as selections from the permanent collection of 20th-century American crafts—are on view in this distinguished building. The Grand Salon is elegantly furnished in the opulent style of the 1860s and 1870s.

Today the museum collects the work of artists who are important in the development of 20th-century American crafts. Changing exhibitions from the permanent collection of some 450 objects of glass, metal, ceramics, wood, and fiber are shown on the second floor. The many artists represented include Anni Albers, Wendell Castle, Dale Chihuly, William Harper, Harvey Littleton, Albert Paley, and Peter Voulkos.

The special exhibition program addresses major issues in American crafts and decorative arts, including sources, influences, and earlier historical traditions. Recent exhibitions have included "Common Beauty in Uncommon Objects: The Legacy of African American Craft Art," "American Wicker," and "Louis Comfort Tiffany."

THE BUILDING

The building itself is a major artistic achievement. Its restoration is in part a result of the effort to preserve the character of the Lafayette Park-Pennsylvania Avenue area near the White House. This handsome structure is a notable example of French Second Empire style. William Wilson Corcoran's monogram and profile portrait appear with the motto, "Dedicated to Art," over the front entrance.

Construction began in 1858, but the Civil War intervened; from 1861 to 1869, the building was a warehouse for military material and the headquarters of the quartermaster general. Although the interior was not completed until 1874, a gala public preview was held in February 1871 with President and Mrs. Ulysses S. Grant presiding over a grand ball to

• **Bruce Mitchell (b. 1949), Star Chamber, walnut burl, 1987 (gift of Jane and Arthur Mason)**

raise additional funds for the Washington Monument.

Corcoran's collections occupied the building from 1874 until 1897, when they were moved to the new Corcoran Gallery of Art nearby. The U.S. Court of Claims used the building for 65 years beginning in 1899.

The Grand Salon, exemplifying the splendor of a sumptuous Victorian salon of the 1860s and 1870s, is among the finest historic interiors in Washington. Its paintings are from the collection of the National Museum of American Art.

• Sidney Ralph Hulter (b. 1954), vase, plate glass, 1990 (gift of the James Renwick Alliance, Anne and Ronald Abramson, Sarah and Edwin Hansen, and museum purchase through the Smithsonian Collections Acquisition Program)

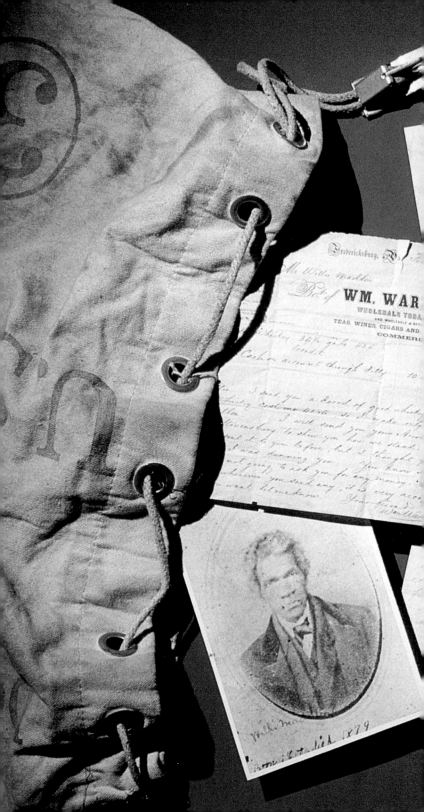

NATIONAL POSTAL MUSEUM

2 Massachusetts Avenue at First Street, NE
In the Washington City Post Office Building next to Union Station
Open daily except December 25, 10 a.m. to 5:30 p.m.
Metro station: Union Station
Smithsonian information: (202) 357-2700
Information recording in Spanish: (202) 633-9126
TTY: (202) 357-1729 (for callers with communication impairments)

As long as civilization has fostered written language, people have relied on mail communication. In 3500 B.C., the Sumerians carried messages inscribed on cuneiform tablets and placed in clay envelopes. Thousands of years later, when the colonists settled North America, they carved mail routes through the unexplored terrain of the Northeast. By 1770, there were 28 post offices in the colonies, 3,057 kilometers (1,900 miles) of post roads, and 75 post riders. Mail was vital in helping

NATIONAL POSTAL MUSEUM

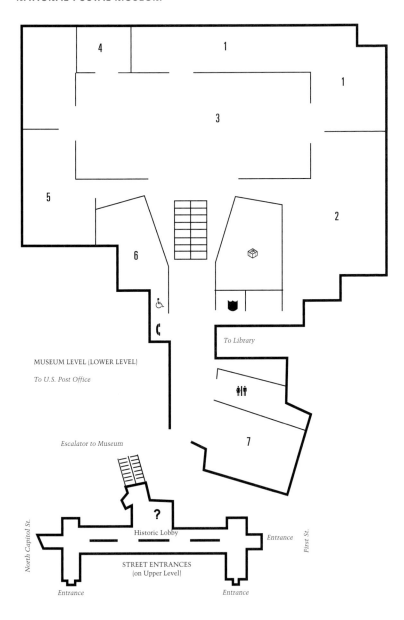

4

1

1

3

5

2

6

♿

☏

MUSEUM LEVEL (LOWER LEVEL)

To Library

To U.S. Post Office

🚻

Escalator to Museum

7

?

North Capitol St.

Historic Lobby

Entrance

First St.

STREET ENTRANCES
(on Upper Level)

Entrance

Entrance

? Information	🚻 Restrooms	1 Binding the Nation
🛡 Security Office	🎁 Museum Shop	2 Customers and Communities
▦ Escalators	☏ Telephones	3 Moving the Mail
♿ Elevators/Accessible Entrance		4 The Art of Cards and Letters
		5 Stamps & Stories
		6 Stamp Store
		7 Discovery Center

ENTRANCE
Enter the lobby of the building and proceed by escalator to the floor level of the museum's 27-meter-(90-foot) high atrium.

INFORMATION DESK
Located off the lobby

TOURS
Free guided walk-in tours are offered weekdays at 11 a.m., 1 p.m., and 2 p.m. and weekends at 11 a.m.and 1 p.m. Confirm tour times at the information desk, or call (202) 357-2700. General and specialized tours may be scheduled for school groups and organizations as well as for visitors with disabilities. At least two weeks' notice is required; call (202) 357-2991.

MUSEUM SHOP
Located near the escalators at the museum entrance, the shop offers posters, T-shirts, stationery, postcards, jewelry, first-day covers, stamp collector kits, stamp- and postal-related souvenirs, books for all ages on postal history subjects and letter collections, and an extensive selection of philatelic publications.

STAMP STORE
Operated by the United States Postal Service, the Stamp Store is located opposite the Museum Shop. Visitors may purchase a variety of current stamps and other commemorative stamp items.

PUBLIC PROGRAMS
Museum programs include postal history and philatelic lectures, panel discussions, performances, and family activities.

DISCOVERY CENTER
This education and activity room offers families an opportunity to work together on Activity Mail Boxes filled with games, puzzles, and hands-on adventures. It is also a setting for public programs and events. Call (202) 357-2991 to confirm hours of operation.

RESEARCH FACILITIES
With more than 40,000 volumes and manuscripts, the museum's library is among the world's largest postal history and philatelic research facilities. The library features a specimen study room, an audiovisual viewing room, and a rare book library. Open by appointment, Monday through Friday from 10 a.m. to 4 p.m.; call (202) 633-9370 to schedule a visit.

U.S. POST OFFICE
Accessible from the main hall of the museum

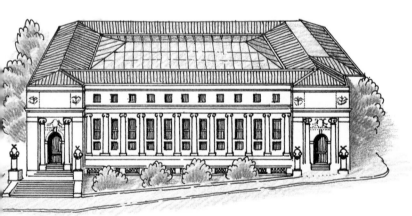

AT A GLANCE

The National Postal Museum is a family-oriented museum that explores the **history of the nation's postal service and celebrates the art of letter writing and the beauty and lore of stamps**. Visitors can travel on the first postal road, open a mailbag, sit in a stagecoach, sort the mail, and create a stamp collection. They can also enjoy more than 30 audiovisual and interactive areas. Changing exhibitions focus on philatelic rarities, specialized and topical stamp collections, U.S. and foreign commemorative stamps, letter-related themes, postcards, greeting cards, and more.

•ABOVE: View of the recently restored lobby of the City Post Office Building, now the walkway to the National Postal Museum.

•RIGHT: A 1911 Wiseman-Cooke, based on the Wright brothers' first plane, hangs from the atrium ceiling along with a 1924 DeHavilland mail plane, and a 1930s Stinson Reliant.

DIRECTOR'S BEST

Each director makes some lasting impact on the collections. I believe that mine is reflected by the array of postal vehicles. From one vehicle in 1984, the museum's collection now includes nearly a dozen significant examples. My personal favorite is an 1851 Concord stagecoach.

—James Bruns, Director, National Postal Museum

the colonies attain the cooperation necessary to the success of the American Revolution. The postal service evolved in tandem with the nation's industrial, technological, and social progress. This unique and inspiring perspective on American history is told in the National Postal Museum.

The museum is located on the lower level of the historic City Post Office Building, designed by Daniel Burnham and built in 1914. It served as the main Washington, D.C., post office from 1914 through 1986. The collection grew out of a donation in 1886 of a sheet of 10-cent Confederate postage stamps. Known for many years as the National Philatelic Collection, this rich collection has grown through generous gifts from individuals and foreign governments, transfers from government agencies, and occasional purchases to include more than 16 million items.

Drawing on its vast collection, the museum has five major exhibition galleries highlighting topics such as the early history of the mail and its rapid

• TOP: A display on the colonial press depicts avenues of mail transportation between England and the newly settled American colonies. Benjamin Franklin contributed to the service and was named Postmaster General of Philadelphia in 1737 by the British Crown. By 1753, he was Postmaster General for all of the colonies under the Crown.

• MIDDLE: Folk art mailboxes in the Rural Free Delivery display in the "Customers and Communities" gallery. People across America show their ingenuity by creating unique customized mailboxes, which can be spotted along rural mail routes.

• BOTTOM: A 1931 Ford Model-A mail truck is on display in the "Moving the Mail" gallery. In 1921, the Post Office began to standardize the postal fleet, and by the 1930s commanded a fleet of more than 8,000 vehicles.

growth as a modern enterprise, the art of letter writing, and the beauty and lore of stamps.

BINDING THE NATION

This gallery traces events from colonial times through the 19th century, stressing the importance of written communication. As early as 1673, regular mail was carried between New York and Boston following Indian trails. Benjamin Franklin, a colonial postmaster for the British government, played a key role in establishing mail service. By 1800, mail was carried over more than 9,000 miles of postal roads. The challenge of developing mail service over long distances is the central theme of "The Expanding Nation," which chronicles the famed Pony Express and the Southern Postal Administration during the Civil War. Interactive video stations invite visitors to create their own postal routes or move mailbags from Philadelphia to New Orleans in the 1850s.

CUSTOMERS AND COMMUNITIES

By the turn of the 20th century, the nation's population was expanding, and so was mail volume and the need for personal mail delivery. Crowded cities and the needs of rural Americans inspired the invention of new delivery systems. Facets of the developing system and its important role in the fabric of the nation are explored using photographs, mail vehicles, a variety of rural mailboxes, and other artifacts.

Parcel post service helped usher in an era of consumerism by the early 20th century that foreshadowed the massive mechanization and automation of mail and the mail order industry. Today, mail service is a vital conduit for business.

MOVING THE MAIL

Faced with the challenge of moving the mail quickly, the postal service looked to trains, automobiles, airplanes, and buses. These means of transportation are the focus of the museum's atrium gallery.

After the Civil War, postal officials began to take advantage of trains for moving and sorting the mail. Railway mail clerks worked the mail while it was being carried between towns. Airmail was established between New York and Chicago in 1918. Few

• ABOVE: The correspondence of the Madden family, an African American family whose letters trace back five generations (1740-1992), was one of a continuing series of letter displays about family histories.

• BELOW: In the "Stamps and Stories" gallery, an in-depth video outlines the complex method of printing stamps. The video display is flanked by two large columns filled with chad, the paper dots left over after stamps are perforated.

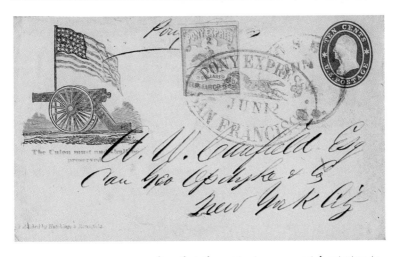

●ABOVE: Pony Express cover, June 1861. The legendary Pony Express lasted only 18 months, but was used widely in its short life. This outstanding cover traces a journey from San Francisco, where a "Running Pony" mark was applied, to the St. Joseph, Missouri post office where it was transported to the New York addressee. Other markings include a $2.00 Wells Fargo & Co. stamp, depicting the charge for use of the Pony Express, on a 10-cent U.S. embossed stamped envelope.

realize that the nation's commercial aviation industry developed from airmail service.

Some of the most ambitious movers of the mail were star route contractors, who were not actually postal employees. Still working today, contractors have delivered mail using everything from mules to motorcycles, including the 1850s Concord-style stagecoach that is on display.

THE ART OF CARDS AND LETTERS

This gallery focuses on letters, which are useful windows into history. Through wartime correspondence from World War I to Operation Desert Storm, one display highlights the efforts of soldiers and their loved ones to maintain ties during war. The many different themes of postcards and greeting cards are playfully examined in another display. Changing exhibits tell the stories of families and friends who are bound together by letters over distance and across time.

STAMPS AND STORIES

Since Great Britain issued the first adhesive postal stamp in 1840, stamps of every subject, shape, and design have been produced for consumer use or as collectibles. Stamps not only serve as proof of postage. They are also miniature works of art, keepsakes, rare treasures, and the workhorses of the automated postal system. Some stamps tell stories, while others contain secrets and hidden meanings.

Highlights of the gallery are rarities from the museum's vast collection, including inverted stamps and unique covers. Videos answer questions about how and why stamps were invented and how they are printed. More than 55,000 stamps are on display, and the selection is rotated every year.

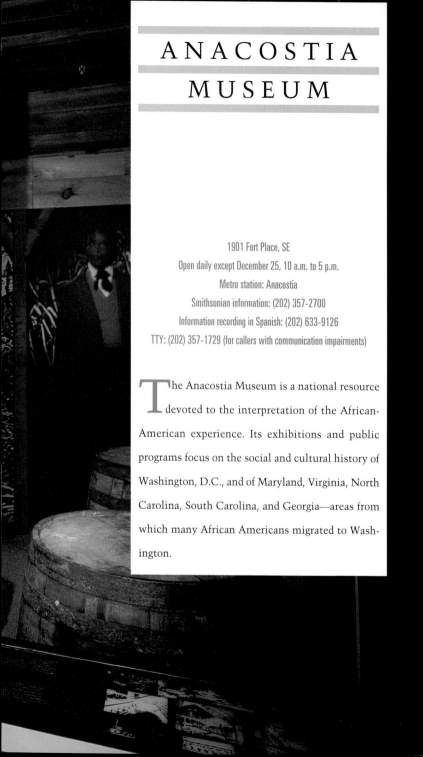

ANACOSTIA
MUSEUM

1901 Fort Place, SE
Open daily except December 25, 10 a.m. to 5 p.m.
Metro station: Anacostia
Smithsonian information: (202) 357-2700
Information recording in Spanish: (202) 633-9126
TTY: (202) 357-1729 (for callers with communication impairments)

The Anacostia Museum is a national resource devoted to the interpretation of the African-American experience. Its exhibitions and public programs focus on the social and cultural history of Washington, D.C., and of Maryland, Virginia, North Carolina, South Carolina, and Georgia—areas from which many African Americans migrated to Washington.

HOW TO GET THERE

The Anacostia Museum is located in a park setting in southeast Washington, with ample parking for cars and buses. Picnic tables and grills are nearby.

By Metrorail and Metrobus: Take the Green Line to the Anacostia station and transfer to the W-1 or W-2 Metrobus to the museum. *By car*: From downtown, take the Southeast Freeway (I-395) to the 11th Street Bridge and exit at Martin Luther King Jr. Avenue. At the fourth traffic light, turn left at Morris Road, and drive up the hill to the museum. *From I-295 south*: Take the Howard Road exit, and turn left on Martin Luther King Jr. Avenue. Turn right at Morris Road, and continue up the hill to the museum.

The Anacostia Museum bus is available for school and community groups. Call (202) 287-3369 for scheduling.

SPECIAL ACTIVITIES AND TOURS

Special activities for adults and children include lectures, workshops, films, and performance events. A calendar of events is available on request. For information, call (202) 287-2060; TTY (202) 357-1729 (for callers with communication impairments). To schedule a tour, call the Education Department, (202) 287-3369.

RESEARCH

The museum's Research Department provides fellowship and internship opportunities to undergraduate and graduate students in African American studies. Internships are also available in the Design and Production, Education, and Public Programs departments. Write to the Intern Coordinator, Anacostia Museum, 1901 Fort Place, SE, Washington, D.C. 20020, or call (202) 287-3369.

MUSEUM SHOP

The Museum Shop features books, posters, compact discs, and other items of African American interest.

AT A GLANCE

Established in 1967 as the nation's first federally funded neighborhood museum, the Anacostia Museum has become a significant community-based cultural resource. Research, exhibition, and education activities focus on the **African American experience in Washington, D.C., and the Upper South** region of Virginia, Maryland, North Carolina, South Carolina, and Georgia.

A revolving exhibition program includes collaborative efforts with the community such as the recent "Black Mosaic: Community, Race, and Ethnicity among Black Immigrants in Washington, D.C." An active community gallery program gives local residents a venue for exhibitions of local history and work by artists from the community. For information about exhibition and program schedules, call (202) 287-2060.

Scholars and researchers find unique opportunities to study African American history and culture at the Anacostia Museum. The museum's collections of archival material, photographs, books, and artifacts reflect neighborhood and city history, women's history, literature, and contemporary community life. Community-based documentation and education efforts sponsored by the museum include the Friends for the Preservation of African American History and Culture and the Unbroken Circle Church Archive Group.

The museum explores contemporary social and community issues as well as popular culture and cultural materials. Special initiatives include the environmental awareness program, the George Washington Carver Nature Trail, and a youth-centered partnership with the Lucy Ellen Moten Elementary School. Annual events include the June celebration of "Juneteenth," the day the slaves in Texas first learned of their freedom.

Research, collection development, and outreach at the museum are models for replication by other community-based museums. An active publications program features brochures, educational materials, and exhibition-related publications.

●PRECEDING PAGES: This installation–from the exhibition "The Real McCoy: African American Invention and Innovation, 1619-1930"–illustrates the open kettle method of making sugar prior to the invention of Norbert Rillieux's multiple-effect vacuum evaporation system.

●ABOVE: Quilt, silk with embroidery, by Kissie Gray; Saudi River, South Carolina, ca. 1855

●OPPOSITE: Dancers perform at the Anacostia Museum's annual Juneteenth Celebration, which commemorates the day that slaves in Texas first learned of their freedom.

NATIONAL ZOOLOGICAL PARK

Entrances: Connecticut Avenue, NW (3000 block between
Cathedral Avenue and Devonshire Place)
Harvard Street and Adams Mill Road intersection
Beach Drive in Rock Creek Park
Open daily except December 25
Grounds open 8 a.m. to 6 p.m. (October 16 to April 14) and
8 a.m. to 8 p.m. (April 15 to October 15)
Animal buildings open 9 a.m. to 4:30 p.m. unless otherwise posted
Metro station: Woodley Park/Zoo
Information recording: (202) 673-4800
Information recording in Spanish: (202) 633-9126
Information desk: (202) 673-4717
TTY: (202) 357-1729 (for callers with communication impairments)

The National Zoo is world famous for the display, breeding, and study of wild animals. Visitors can see most of the animals in naturalistic settings that comfortably house social groups approximating those found in the wild.

HOW TO GET THERE

The Zoo is three blocks from the Woodley Park/Zoo Metro-rail station and is accessible by Metrobus. For Metro information, call (202) 637-7000 or TTY (202) 638-3780. Admission is free. Limited pay parking is available on Zoo lots. Bus passenger discharge, pickup, and limited free bus parking are available.

WHERE TO EAT

The Zoo has a variety of fast-food facilities. Picnic areas are located throughout the grounds, but no outdoor cooking is permitted.

TOURS

Self-guided Audio Safari Tours may be rented from information stations. Guided weekend tours of Zoo highlights for families, individuals, or groups are available with a three-week advance reservation. Call Friends of the National Zoo, (202) 673-4955.

SERVICES

The Zoo has ramped building entrances and restroom facilities for nonambulatory visitors. Strollers may be rented in season for a small fee. A limited number of wheelchairs are available to borrow. Zoo police provide lost-and-found service and a refuge for lost children.

GIFT SHOPS AND BOOKSTORE

Unique zoo-oriented articles—souvenirs, postcards, books, T-shirts, and art objects—are for sale.

FEEDING TIMES

The giant panda is fed at 11 a.m. outdoors (weather permitting) and 3 p.m. indoors. Feeding times for other animals vary according to the season and the keeper work schedule. The big cats and bears are not fed in exhibit areas.

HELPFUL HINTS

Consider using public transportation; Zoo parking lots often fill up early in the warm months. Wear comfortable clothing and shoes. Do not overexert in hot weather; find a comfortable place in the shade to rest. Plan to visit early in the day or in the evening during warmer months, when it is less crowded and the animals are more active. Fall and early winter are great times to visit the Zoo.

SOME RULES TO FOLLOW

Pets are not permitted in the park, except certified-assistance animals. Stay on your side of the guard rail. Zoo animals are wild and easily excited. The area between the guard rail and the enclosure barrier is for your safety and the safety of the animals. Please do not feed the animals. The Zoo provides excellent balanced diets. Additional feeding is unhealthy for the animals. Please do not ride bicycles or any skates in the park. Earphones must be used with radios and tape players.

AT A GLANCE

A **panda from China, infant lowland gorillas, Indonesian Komodo dragon lizards, golden lion tamarins, the Pollinarium exhibit**, and the **Amazonia rainforest habitat** are just a few of the attractions at the National Zoo. Each year millions of visitors come to this scenic and extensive park to see these and others of the approximately 5,500 animals of nearly 480 species on exhibit in naturalistic settings.

The 163-acre biological park is set in the picturesque, sharply cut stream valley of Rock Creek. Steep, wooded hillsides form backdrops for many animal exhibits, and a variety of native and ornamental plants—especially plants that attract butterflies—add to the beauty of the Zoo's landscape. All the animal trails begin and end at Olmsted Walk, the park's central walkway connecting the 18 major animal exhibit complexes. It is named for the renowned landscape architect Frederick Law Olmsted, who created the original design for the National Zoo.

Of course, the 5,500 animals are the focus of attention at the Zoo. A fine variety of vertebrate species, representing the most spectacular forms of land animals, make up most of the collection. Invertebrate and aquatic species as well as biological communities help provide a more comprehensive picture of animal life for Zoo visitors. Educational graphics, learning carts, and learning labs enrich public understanding of the park's animals and plants.

EXHIBITS

Amazonia, the largest exhibit to open at the National Zoo in the past 50 years, features a tropical rainforest. A lush forest habitat complete with a stream is home to a diverse array of free-ranging amphibians, mammals, and birds. Huge aquariums hold schools of exotic fish. Visitors can also walk through a reproduction of a biologist's field station in the tropics.

The Reptile Discovery Center, an interactive, educational exhibit designed especially for families with school-age children, explores the biology of reptiles and amphibians. Visitors are encouraged to use listening, visual, and smelling skills to investigate these animals' feeding and communication strategies and learn about their anatomy.

● ABOVE: **The Amazonia exhibit, a 15,000 square-foot rainforest, includes a cascading river with tropical fish, 358 species of plants, and dozens of free-ranging animals.**

● LEFT: **Only about 1,000 giant pandas survive in the wild today. Giant panda Hsing-Hsing came to the National Zoo in 1972 as a gift from the People's Republic of China.**

● RIGHT: **Invertebrates make up 99% of the animal species on Earth. Learn more about these fascinating creatures without backbones in the Invertebrate Exhibit at the Zoo.**

DIRECTOR'S BEST

• *The Invertebrate Exhibit*
Among the stars of this exhibit are a giant octopus, cuttlefish, anemones, corals, and web-building spiders. The giant octopus is fed several times a day and is a wonderful sight to behold. I've seen it open a screw-top jar with a shrimp inside.

• *The Small Mammal House*
Full of delightful animals from small cats to dwarf mongooses. My favorites are the fennec foxes, from the deserts of the Middle East.

• *Reptile Discovery Center*
Our reptile house is now an interactive exploratorium.

• *The Wetlands Exhibit*
Outside the bird house are five great pools containing a wide range of waterfowl and wading birds. This is a marvelously relaxing vista where one can escape from the urban jungle.

• *Otters in the Valley*
Otters are my favorite animals. In Beaver Valley we have a group of more than a dozen Asian small-clawed otters. When they're active, they are a delight to the eye, and we illuminate their den so that you can see them sleeping.

—Michael Robinson, Director, National Zoological Park

The recently renovated Monkey House now features Think Tank, an interactive exhibit that encourages animals to demonstrate their cognitive skills while visitors watch. The Orangutan Transport System, a series of towers connected by cables, allows the orangutans to travel between the Great Ape House and Think Tank.

The Elephant House, with both indoor and outdoor exhibit areas, is home to Asian and African elephants, Masai giraffes, Nile and Pygmy hippopotamuses, and the greater one-horned Asiatic rhinoceros.

A colorful array of invertebrate life—including insects, sponges, sea stars, mollusks, crabs, and other animals without backbones—is on view in the Invertebrate Exhibit. The Pollinarium, a glass-enclosed addition to the exhibit, illustrates the evolution, beauty, and mechanics of pollination.

In the Great Flight Cage, visitors can stroll among species of the more than 150 types of birds on display in the Zoo.

The Education/Administration Building has an auditorium where lectures and other programs are held, a bookstore, and a public educational facility called ZOOlab, open Friday through Sunday from 10 a.m. to 1 p.m.

•OPPOSITE TOP:
California sea lions basking in the sun.

•OPPOSITE MIDDLE:
Golden lion tamarins became an endangered species in their native Brazil as development destroyed parts of their unique forest home. This is one of a large colony of the colorful little monkeys bred at the Zoo.

•OPPOSITE BOTTOM: In the Wetlands Exhibit, Zoo visitors enter a natural waterfowl habitat teeming with life.

•ABOVE: The Cheetah Conservation Station was established to study cheetah behavior as part of a massive effort to save this endangered species.

CONSERVATION AND RESEARCH

There is a great deal more to the National Zoo than the animals on public exhibit. Behind the scenes, scientists conduct conservation and research programs in animal behavior, ecology, and propagation. At the animal hospital and scientific research building on the Zoo grounds and at the Conservation and Research Center in Front Royal, Virginia, zoologists are constantly working to learn more about wild animal ecology and behavior to improve the care of animals in the Zoo and facilitate their breeding. On the 3,150-acre tract in Virginia, particular emphasis is on long-range breeding programs for many rare species, with the participation of other zoos. In recent years, the National Zoo has also sponsored and taken part in scientific programs in many parts of the world. These programs have

• ABOVE LEFT: The Komodo dragon is the world's largest lizard—adult males can exceed 10 feet and weigh as much as 200 pounds. The Zoo is successfully breeding this highly endangered species.

• ABOVE RIGHT: A red wolf enjoys the snow at the National Zoo.

• OPPOSITE: Each gorilla birth at the National Zoo builds a firmer foundation for the survival of this magnificent, endangered species.

contributed greatly to knowledge of the biology and behavior of wild animals.

HISTORY

Almost from its beginning, the Smithsonian Institution received gifts of live animals, but there was no zoo in Washington, D.C., then. Some were sent to zoos elsewhere; some were kept on the National Mall, and over the years a sizable menagerie accumulated outside the Smithsonian Castle. In 1889, Congress established the National Zoological Park at the urging of Samuel Pierpont Langley, third secretary of the Smithsonian, and naturalist William T. Hornaday, who was particularly concerned with saving the American bison from extinction. Six bison were among the animals transferred from the Mall to the newly created National Zoo.

Animal collecting expeditions in the 1920s and 1930s, along with gifts from individuals and foreign governments and exchanges with other zoos, have all contributed to the Zoo's population. As the nation's "official zoo," the National Zoological Park is host to visitors from around the nation and the world.

Today the National Zoo is evolving into a new kind of zoo: the BioPark. This vision of the modern zoo focuses on the natural interdependence of life on Earth and integrates elements of the natural sciences, human cultures, and the arts.

FRIENDS OF THE NATIONAL ZOO

Friends of the National Zoo (FONZ) is a nonprofit membership organization of families and individuals who participate in special Zoo programs and support the goals of the National Zoo in conservation, education, and research. FONZ members serve as Zoo guides, help in animal behavior studies, receive wildlife publications, and participate in special events. Proceeds from the concessions operated by FONZ are used to further education and research programs.

COOPER-HEWITT NATIONAL DESIGN MUSEUM

2 East 91st Street (at Fifth Avenue), New York, New York

Hours: Tuesday, 10 a.m. to 9 p.m.; Wednesday through Saturday,

10 a.m. to 5 p.m.; Sunday, noon to 5 p.m.

Closed Monday and major holidays (Christmas, New Year's Day,

Memorial Day, Fourth of July, Labor Day, Thanksgiving)

Information: (212) 860-6868

Information recording in Spanish: (202) 633-9126

TTY: (202) 357-1729 (for callers with communication impairments)

Cooper-Hewitt National Design Museum explores both the processes and the products of design—a fundamental activity that includes objects as common as a paper cup, as distinctive as a crystal goblet, or as complex as a city. The museum examines the influence these objects have on our daily lives and how they shape and are shaped by our culture. Its broad concerns encompass fields as varied as urban planning, architecture, industrial

NOTE: Museum galleries may close temporarily due to a renovation project scheduled for completion in September 1996. Please call the museum for information.

INFORMATION DESK

Located just inside the main entrance

TOURS

Guided tours are available for groups of six or more by advance arrangement with the Programs Office; call (212) 860-6871. Free gallery talks are scheduled for current exhibitions.

MUSEUM SHOP

The Design Museum Shop, located near the main entrance, offers exhibition catalogues; posters; slides; postcards; books on the decorative arts, architecture, and design; books relating to the museum's collections and current exhibitions; jewelry; ceramics; and gift items.

EDUCATIONAL PROGRAMS

The museum has an active calendar of workshops, courses, lectures, study tours, films, and seminars throughout the year, including programs for all ages and the entire family. Free summer concerts are scheduled in the Arthur Ross Terrace and Garden. Special children's programs are available for school groups. With the New School/Parsons School of Design, Cooper-Hewitt offers a two-year program leading to a master of arts degree in the history of decorative arts.

RESEARCH FACILITIES

The museum's library contains more than 50,000 volumes, including 6,000 rare volumes. The library's picture collections include material on color, pattern, textiles, symbols, advertising, and interior and industrial design. It also has graphic and industrial design archives. Object study centers are available for textiles, drawings and prints, and wallcoverings. The research facilities are open by appointment; call (212) 860-6883.

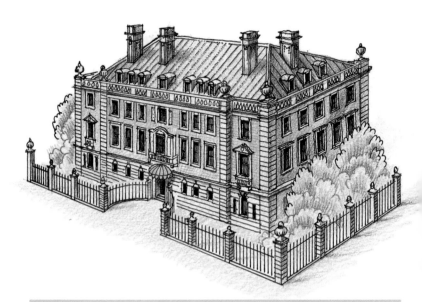

AT A GLANCE

Cooper-Hewitt National Design Museum presents changing exhibitions of historic and contemporary design. It has impressive collections of **furniture, metalwork, glass, ceramics, jewelry, woodwork, embroidery, woven and printed textiles, lace, and wallcoverings.** The museum also has one of the largest collections of drawings in the United States, a large collection of prints— including examples of **architectural drawings, advertising, fashion design, theater design, and interior design**—and an important specialized library.

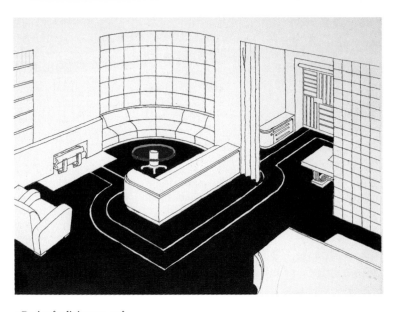

• Design for living room of
Eleanor Hutton Rand,
Donald Deskey (Ameri-
can), 1934

design, landscape design, interior design, textiles,
fashion, theater arts, advertising, graphic arts, and
crafts.

Through its diverse programs, the National Design Museum encourages "good design," fosters a
better understanding of the design process, stimulates discussion in related fields, and increases dia-
logue between audience and designer. The museum
pursues these goals by making the collections available for study and display, providing educational
programs for professionals and the public, present-
ing exhibitions, issuing publications, and holding
conferences keyed to significant design issues.

HISTORY

Cooper-Hewitt was founded in 1897 by the Hewitt
sisters, granddaughters of New York manufacturer
and philanthropist Peter Cooper. The Cooper Union
Museum for the Arts of Decoration, as it was called,
was a working laboratory, freely available to a broad
public and accessible as a reference center for de-
signers, scholars, and students. Threatened with
closure because of the financial problems of its par-
ent institution (Cooper Union for the Advancement
of Science and Art), the museum's supporters saved
it by mounting a major fund-raising drive. The collections were transferred to the Smithsonian in
1968, and the name was changed to acknowledge
its founders and heritage. In 1972, the museum and
its collections found a permanent home when the
Carnegie Corporation donated the historic 1902
Georgian Revival mansion, built as the private home

DIRECTOR'S BEST

I am continually amazed at the extent to which design has an imapct on our daily lives. At Cooper-Hewitt, we encourage people to think in new ways about ordinary objects—those things we often take for granted. Our collections are so diverse and so intriguing; each object in our collection makes a statement and shows us another solution to a design problem. From Renaissance jewelry to the work of some of the most ingenious ceramists and potters; from historic drawings of English interiors to the working drawings of contemporary architects; from 17th-century hand-printed French wallpapers to mass-produced papers of the 1950s; from English samplers to metallic fabrics; it would be hard to choose a favorite, or even a few! Instead, these varied holdings remind me that design connects all disciplines of study as well as individuals and societies.

--Dianne H. Pilgrim, Director, Cooper-Hewitt National Design Museum

of industrialist Andrew Carnegie, and the small neighboring townhouse to the Smithsonian. Cooper-Hewitt reopened to the public in 1976.

EXHIBITIONS

Cooper-Hewitt produces a continuing program of about 12 changing exhibitions each year. Although the collection is not on permanent display in the museum's galleries, exhibitions and publications frequently explore its specific strengths. To convey the universal character of design, the museum has exhibited items not usually seen in a museum setting. Special attention is given to showing objects in new and unexpected contexts. Parts of installations, or even entire exhibitions, invite visitor participation, stimulating thought about the practical aspects of design. The museum also has explored crosscultural patterns in design history and addressed environmental and social concerns as they affect and are affected by design.

• OPPOSITE: **Block-printed cotton fabric, Soehnée l'Ainé et Cie (France), ca. 1795**

• ABOVE: **Ceramic bowl, Elsa Rady (American), 1984**

COLLECTIONS

More than 250,000 design and decorative arts objects form a collection of enormous scope and diversity. It spans most of the world's cultures over 3,000 years, with the greatest emphasis on Western cultures of the past 400 years. Holdings range from the utilitarian to the fine arts and are divided into four major curatorial departments: decorative arts, drawings and prints, textiles, and wallcoverings. Particular areas of strength are the 17th through the mid-19th century. The museum is expanding its collection with acquisitions of works of the late 19th and 20th centuries, including examples of contemporary urban and industrial design. A department of contemporary design mounts exhibitions on 20th-century design.

The collection was assembled with a singular purpose: to provide visual information for the study of design. The objects are divided by medium and technique rather than by culture, period, or historical chronology. To ease research, the museum provides ready cross-references between the collections and the library.